SOCIALIST HISTO

SOCIALIST HISTORY
OCCASIONAL PUBLICATION No. 35

BRITISH
SOCIALISM
IN THE
EARLY 1900s

FRANK TANNER

2014

Published by the Socialist History Society 2014, from an unpublished manuscript originally completed in 1956.

Designed and typeset by SHS, 2014

ISBN 978-0-9930104-0-8

Henry Mayers Hyndman (1842-1921)
Source: Lee and Archbold, *Social-Democracy in Britain*

Contents

Foreword	...	2
1. British Socialism in the Early 1900s	...	6
2. A Changing Political Scene	...	15
3. Rise of the Labour Party	...	17
4. The Suffrage Agitation	...	25
5. The Fight for the Unemployed	...	38
6. The Social-Democratic Federation in Action	...	59
7. The Internationalism of the SDF	...	71
8. The Birth of the British Socialist Party	...	80
9. The Great Strikes	...	85
10. Factitious Unity	...	97
11. How British Social Democracy Worked	...	109
12. Re-affiliation at Last	...	124
Editors' notes	...	130

Foreword

Frank Tanner (1887-1958) was involved in the socialist, and subsequently the Communist, movement from his early twenties until his death. He joined the Social-Democratic Party (previously Social-Democratic Federation) in Brixton in 1908, moved over with the SDP into the British Socialist Party in 1911, and in 1920 was a delegate from West Islington BSP at the first Unity Convention which formed the Communist Party of Great Britain. Within a few years of joining the SDP, he was writing articles for the party press. In 1911 and 1912, he published *Socialism and Individual Liberty*, and *Socialism and Human Nature* with the party's Twentieth Century Press. He took an active part in inner-party debates; according to a report in *Justice*, in December 1913, Tanner passionately opposed the proposal from the BSP executive to affiliate to the Labour Party, a position also taken by Herbert Burrows.

However, Tanner's career as a party publicist was short. His last pamphlet, *The Land Grabbers*, was published by the newly-formed CPGB in 1921. Thereafter, he seems to have faded into obscurity, at least as far as his published output is concerned. There is little mention of him in the CPGB press, either as a writer, speaker or party propagandist. He stood for the CP as a local election candidate in Wandsworth in 1922, and served as branch secretary of various South London CP branches in the 1920s, but after that the trail seems to go cold. His occupation in the mid-1920s was listed as "clerk", which probably gave little scope for the sort of militant industrial activity which sometimes brought communists to public attention.

Nonetheless, Frank Tanner clearly remained a loyal and engaged member of the CPGB throughout. When, in the mid-1950s, the CPGB started to take its own history more seriously, with the beginnings of a party archive and the attention of the CP Historians' Group (CPHG) turning towards the party itself, Tanner contributed his researches and reminiscences on pre-WW1 social democracy to the party's efforts. His research was used in the CPHG pamphlet *Some Dilemmas for Marxists 1900-1914* (*Our History* No. 4, Winter 1956).

Tanner's memoir is especially valuable as we have few contemporary records of SDF politics other than H. M. Hyndman's own memoirs. Tanner provides a narrative of the political organisation at national level, but also of the political activities of social democrats in South London, notably Brixton and Camberwell, which have not been otherwise recorded. This local perspective is largely missing from the historical record, with the exception of Andrew Rothstein's study of the

2

Hackney and Kingsland branch between 1903 and 1906 (*Our History*, No. 19, 1960).

There is a considerably larger secondary literature on the SDF. Its official history, H. W. Lee and E. Archbold's *Social-Democracy in Britain*, was published by the last remnants of the reconstituted SDF in 1935. A full-length political biography of the party's founder appeared in 1961: Chushichi Tsuzuki, *H. M. Hyndman and British Socialism*; this work remains the standard study of Hyndman. More recently, we have Martin Crick's *History of the Social-Democratic Federation* (1994) and Graham Johnson's study of *Social Democratic Politics in Britain 1881-1911* (2002). There are also more specialist works such as Karen Hunt's 1996 *Equivocal Feminists* which considers the debate within the SDF on "the woman question", as well as memoirs by SDF leaders such as Will Thorne and Dora Montefiore. Some of these works refer to the contribution of SDF branches to national organisation and national debates. Aspects of SDF history have also been considered in articles. The early years are covered in Mark Bevir's "The British Social Democratic Federation 1880-1885" (*International Review of Social History*, 37/2, 1992), while the SDF's work among the unemployed is discussed in Alan J. Kidd, "The Social Democratic Federation and Popular Agitation amongst the Unemployed in Edwardian Manchester" (*International Review of Social History*, 29/3, 1984).

The SDF has been the occasional subject of new doctoral research. David Murray Young, *People, place and party: the social democratic federation 1884-1911* (unpublished PhD thesis, Durham University, 2003), is a study of the membership and activity of the SDF branches in London, although neither Tanner nor his memoir is mentioned in this thesis. The records of the Brixton and Camberwell branches do not seem to have survived, though the account book of the nearby Peckham and Dulwich branch has. The internationalist group within the later SDF/BSP is the subject of David Burke's *Theodore Rothstein and the Russian Political Emigre Influence on the British Labour Movement 1884-1920*, (unpublished PhD thesis, University of Greenwich, 1997).

Frank Tanner's memoir was submitted on 1 May 1956 to one of the party's most prominent ideologists, James Klugmann, who was soon to be given the job of writing the CPGB's official history. A copy came into the possession of Bill Moore, a founder member of the CP Historians' Group and a long-standing full-time party official in Yorkshire, who passed it over to the Socialist History Society shortly before his death in 2008.

Almost sixty years after it was first written, Tanner's account now enters the public domain. We are publishing it more or less "as is". The only changes to the original are corrections to a handful of grammatical errors or typos, and modernisation of the orthography – the original has lots of terms capitalised which now look rather strange. Here and there we have inserted explanatory notes, but editorial intervention has been kept to a bare minimum.

This pamphlet is both a piece of historical writing, and a historical artefact in itself. It reflects the assumptions and ideas of a very particular moment in communist history – early 1956. This was just before the CPGB was battered by the political storm which was set off by Nikita Khrushchev's "Secret Speech" to the 20th CPSU Congress and subsequent events in Poland and Hungary. By the end of that year, the party was suffering a mass exodus of members and the loss of its near-monopoly of organised Marxism in Britain, with the beginnings of the New Left and a certain upsurge in British Trotskyism. By 1960 the unity of the "international communist movement" would be irrevocably shattered. But in early 1956, it was still possible to assume that communist parties all around the world were the natural, historically necessary expression of organised Marxism, and that earlier Marxist bodies were in certain respects mere forerunners of communism, theoretically and politically incomplete. To his great credit, Tanner does not push that line too hard in his account of British social democracy, but the assumption is certainly there.

In places, the language very much reflects both the time it was written, and the intended audience of CPGB members. The Bolshevik faction of Russian social democracy is "the party of Lenin and Stalin", and phrases like "Bruce Glasier, whom we would describe as a centrist" occasionally crop up. But this orientation towards a party readership also conditions one of the great merits of this work – Tanner was at pains to rehabilitate the SDF, at least partially. He sought to challenge a stereotype which presented it as merely a dogmatic, largely propagandist organisation led by a wealthy egotist (Hyndman) with chauvinistic and imperialistic proclivities. Tanner's account, while not denying the SDF's weaknesses, lays stress on the practical activism, particularly around housing and unemployment, undertaken by SDF branches. Hyndman as a figure does not emerge particularly well, but Tanner makes it clear that the SDF was always much more than just Hyndman.

Tanner was clearly a careful and assiduous researcher, despite one or two slips (which are indicated in the endnotes). It is unfortunate that he did not provide full bibliographical references for his sources, although in many cases anyone with the time and inclination can follow them up. Overall, although Tanner's history is very dated, we still consider it a useful addition to the literature on British social democracy.

4

It is not merely a study of documents, but also the recollections of someone who was directly involved, with the first-person immediacy which that brings. Moreover, its age and provenance makes it almost a kind of primary source in its own right – a glimpse of how the socialist politics of a century ago were perceived almost sixty years ago.

Francis King
Duncan Bowie

Author's note on the front page of the MS:

May 1st 1956
This manuscript was made and produced by Frank Tanner of 79 Amesbury Avenue, Brixton, SW2 and was sent to J. Klugmann of Education Dept.

1. British Socialism in the early 1900s

The socialist movement in Britain during the first decade of the present century was a movement almost as much sideways as forwards. For its many groupings from which members passed continuously from one to another were a constant source of astonishment to foreign comrades, accustomed as they were to a single mass party covering all trends. Yet, as Harry Quelch once remarked "There was as much *floating* Socialism in Britain as in any other country."

The fragmentary nature of *organised* British socialism at this time is partly explained by the federal basis of the political Labour movement which as from 1900 *automatically* organised the affiliated TU membership and made any further political organisation on their part appear somewhat superfluous. Hence the importance of parties with an avowed socialist objective, which, based on personal membership, appealed mainly to enthusiasts and theorists.

The relative influence and effectiveness of the various bodies which sought to make and organise British socialists 50 years ago is, of course, a controversial subject. Nevertheless, it is simpler to make an assessment when viewing the situation from a distance of half a century. At any rate, here is mine for what it is worth.

The largest numerically and probably the most influential socialist body (apart from whether its influence was good or bad) was the Independent Labour Party. It had played an important part in the formation of the Labour Representation Committee (by which name the present Labour Party was first known) and was actually active in moulding the latter's policy when formed. The three leading figures in the ILP – Keir Hardie, Ramsay MacDonald and Philip Snowden, together with Arthur Henderson, were at this time also the leading lights of the LRC.

Keir Hardie had already won fame as a working-class pioneer in Parliament where his proletarian style and contempt for Parliamentary conventions formed a refreshing contrast to the correct bearing of his colleagues, but in the early 1900s he was showing signs of toning down. Snowden and MacDonald were never anything but orthodox Parliamentarians and opportunists.

The ILP leadership rejected the class struggle and paid little attention to theory. In so far as they had any theory at all, it was one of gradualness plus the conception that human society was like a sick man needing medical attention and socialists were the doctors. (Note MacDonald's appeal for a "Doctor's Mandate" many years later). Their approach to social problems was ethical and sentimental rather than scientific and, with the exception of a few sound Marxists, the mentality of the membership as a whole reflected that of their leaders.

Needless to say, this theoretical weakness and mental confusion was not inconsistent with a great deal of sound educational work and practical achievement in the streets and on local councils. Genuine workers may deny the class struggle in the abstract but cannot help acting upon it when confronted in practice with straight class issues.

Similar in outlook but much more select as to membership was the Fabian Society which described itself as a "Society of Socialists" and derived its name from the tactics of Fabius Maximus, a Roman guerrilla leader who, while avoiding pitched battles, harried the Carthaginian invaders of Italy for many years. Hence, they rejected completely the conception of a class struggle with its implication of open conflict and pursued a policy of "permeating" existing organisations in the hope of undermining them from within. Thus a number of Fabians had managed to get elected to Parliament and local councils as Liberals or Progressives (e.g. L. Chiozza-Money MP and Sidney Webb LCC) notwithstanding the fact that the society had been affiliated to the Labour Party since its inception.

Fabians were especially active in local government affairs where their concentration on the development of municipal trading and enterprise gained for them the rather dubious title of "Gas and Water Socialists". As a result of much painstaking research the society published numerous pamphlets, mainly of a factual and statistical character. The famous *Fabian Tracts* had a wide circulation and proved of great service to propagandists of all trends.

Somewhat nebulous in character but of very great influence was the readership as well as the network of organisations associated with the popular weekly *Clarion*. This was attached to no particular party and, in consequence, was the least sectarian of the socialist organs with probably the biggest circulation. Its nearest approach to dogmatism was a passionate insistence that Liberals and Tories were equally the enemies of the workers. The editor, Robert Blatchford, had already won immortal fame as the most popular and widely read socialist writer of his day, the penny editions of his *Merrie England* with its rugged simplicity of appeal, reached a far wider public than any other socialist publication.

The weakness of Blatchford's writings lay in their complete lack of scientific basis – a fact of which he was rather proud than otherwise. He did not disagree with Marx but boasted that he had never read him and never intended to. "I don't know the man" he once said, "my socialism is British not German made". This narrow nationalism was to lead at a later stage to his socialist undoing. Nonetheless, in his heyday he and his paper constituted an enormous asset to British socialism.

The *Clarion* hammered away week after week at the broad truths common to all schools of socialist thought and its tone was one of toleration and good fellowship reminiscent of William Morris. Its subsidiary bodies gave invaluable help to all sections of the movement. The bodies referred to consisted of (1) The "Clarion Fellowship" which organised social activities - dances, clubs, etc. (2) the "Clarion Scouts" – groups of cyclists who carried the socialist Gospel to the remotest villages and (3) the "Clarion Vans" which conducted missions in the more crowded areas. (These were usually run jointly with the local ILP and SDF).

The oldest, though not the biggest, socialist body in Britain at the commencement of the century (its membership was probably about half that of the ILP) was the Social-Democratic Federation (Social-Democratic Party as from 1907). Since, with all its shortcomings, the SDF was the nearest approach to the ancestor of our present Communist Party, a Marxist analysis of its tendencies and composition calls for a more detailed treatment than that given to the other parties.

First, it should be borne in mind that the term "Social-Democratic" did not at this time signify, as it does today, treachery and betrayal of the workers' cause. It was the official designation of most of the continental socialist parties, including that of Lenin and Stalin. On the other hand, "social democracy" was not the orthodox type of "British" socialism but stood in the public mind for political militancy.

Though affiliated to the LRC on its formation, the SDF broke away a year or two later, after failing to get the constitution amended to permit of the proclamation of socialism as Labour's final objective. Thereafter British social democracy remained in the political wilderness until 1914.

Alone of the larger socialist organisations in Britain, the SDF claimed to be Marxist. It was a claim that could only be partially justified and indeed the same must be said of all professed Marxists in those days. For what then passed for Marxism consisted of (1) acceptance of the class struggle (2) a rigid insistence on the theory of surplus value and (3) a somewhat over-simplified version of the materialist conception of history. Little was known, let alone understood, by British socialists of dialectics, the functions of the state or the nature of modern imperialism.

The explanation of these limitations is simple enough. The only Marxist classics which elaborated on dialectical materialism and the state were not available to British readers and even if they had been our working-class had not felt the force of the state machine sufficiently to realise the importance, to them, of the somewhat fragmentary passages contained in *Civil War in France* and *Critique of the Gotha Programme*. As for imperialism, the theory had yet to be worked out by Lenin. The tendency was to regard it as something incidental to the earlier colonising capitalist states – glorified nationalism accompanied by crude plunder – rather than an essential stage of capitalism in general, bringing with it the certainty, failing the prior breakdown of the system, of a war for the re-division of the world.

The SDF was not opposed to reforms as such. Indeed its programme contained a lengthy list of them, thereby provoking much scornful comment from ultra-left critics. Yet, it was not itself entirely free from an "impossibilist" (or what to-day would be called "infantile leftist") trend manifested in (1) an overemphasis of the ultimate socialist aim at the expense of the immediate practical steps necessary to reach it (2) undue insistence that only socialists can help forward socialism and (3) a strong tendency to lump together all non-socialist workers as a compact reactionary mass.

Despite these weaknesses, some vigorous campaigns on immediate issues – especially those dealing with unemployment relief and school feeding – were, in fact, waged during this period. Also, there is ample evidence that on issues connected with foreign affairs, social democrats were not usually slow in rising to the occasion. A case in point is the prompt mobilisation of the membership for protest against the judicial murder of the Spanish Republican leader, Ferrer, by the government of King Alfonso.

Let us now take a look at some of the leading personalities connected with British social democracy half a century ago.

The first name that springs to mind in this connection is that of the irrepressible H. M. Hyndman, orator and author. An imposing platform figure, reminding one of Moses, he would clutch his patriarchal beard when making a telling debating point. Never disguising, but rather glorying in the fact that he lived on shares in an armament firm, he never tired of jeering at the workers for presenting his class with the main fruits of their labour. As regards theory, Hyndman might be termed a semi-Marxist, i.e. he accepted with enthusiasm Marx's economic analyses of capitalism while contending that in politics Marx was "more often wrong than right". (Marx, by the way, regarded him as an adventurer and continually referred to him as "that fellow Hyndman"). Hyndman's chief works were *Economics of Socialism* and *Economic Crises of the Nineteenth Century*, both profound and scholarly studies; but it is probable that the published reports of his debates with Bradlaugh and Henry George were more widely read.

On the other hand, it would be vain to deny that the "Grand Old Man of Socialism" was arrogant, autocratic and politically unscrupulous. The sordid episode of "Tory Gold" in the early '80s of last century was still being talked about in the late 1900s when he and Blatchford were commencing their campaign for more arms to meet the "German Menace".

A very different type was Harry Quelch (editor of *Justice*) – a real proletarian who began life as a packer in Cannon Street. Early in the century he earned the gratitude of the Russian social democrats by placing his already cramped editorial office in Clerkenwell Green at the disposal of Lenin and Stalin during their stay in London. In 1907, while attending the Stuttgart Congress of the Second International, he shocked the governments of the world by referring to the Hague "Peace" Conference as a "Thieves' Supper" and was promptly expelled from Germany.

With his sledge-hammer logic and pawky humour Quelch was equally effective as speaker and journalist, his weekly column in *Justice* under the pseudonym of "Tatler" and his short pamphlet *Economics of Labour* being especially popular. In addition to his absorbing activities in the SDF he found time to play a large part in the wider labour movement, more particularly in the work of the London Trades Council of which for some years he was Chairman.

With the possible exception of Hyndman, the greatest literary figure in the SDF at this time was E. Belfort Bax, collaborator with William Morris in compiling the "Socialist Catechism", and author of innumerable books and essays on every aspect of socialist thought – economic, political, historical and philosophical.[1] From his writings it is clear that Bax was not a dialectical materialist but, despite this, his biting criticisms of bourgeois manners and morals are a joy to read.

Probably Bax's greatest service to the movement lay in his historical works, particularly those dealing with the French Revolution and the Paris Commune which presented these earth-shaking events to British readers in an entirely new light. Special mention in this respect must be made of his biography of Jean-Paul Marat which struck a decisive blow at the philistine legend of a bloody inhuman monster and introduced the Peoples' Friend.

Bax's greatest weakness was his antagonism (at least in theory) to the female sex which amounted to an obsession. Not only did he deny that women were oppressed but actually maintained that they were in a privileged position – a theme elaborated in his *Legal Subjection of Men* (not one of his best efforts).

Will Thorne MP was the only SDFer to sit in Parliament and even he was never elected on a straight socialist ticket. He was several times returned as a candidate of the Labour Party being the nominee of the Gas Workers' Union (since absorbed into the NUG&MW) This did not, however, prevent him from proclaiming in unmistakable terms in his election addresses his *personal* views as a socialist.

Ben Tillett, already famous for his leadership in the great Dock Strike of 1889, was a member of the SDF but took no great part in moulding its policy, his responsibilities to the TU movement absorbing most of his energies. But his unusual gifts of oratory made him a favourite figure at meetings and demonstrations.

By way of contrast, H. W. Lee, the Secretary, was a modest but very capable little man who seldom appeared on public platforms. On the other hand there was hardly a job from distributing leaflets to editing the party organ which he did not at some time undertake in the course of his long period of service. Some years later he helped to compile a history of British social democracy.

J. F. Green, the genial Treasurer, was a man of many social accomplishments who, with his wife ran a sort of salon at their house in Herne Hill. Among the bright young people who fore-gathered there were Herbert Morrison, Eleanor Goodrich (recently Mayor of Wandsworth) and Cicely Cook (President of the International Women's Co-op Guild).

Edith Lanchester (mother of Elsa Lanchester) had created a sensation in 1894 when she was forcibly confined to an asylum by her relatives following her declared intention of living with a man without undergoing a marriage ceremony. In the same year she ran for the London School Board on a programme which in certain respects might serve as a model for Communist Party candidates today. (It contained demands for improved playgrounds and smaller classes.) Edith's main sphere of activity in the 1900s was the Socialist Sunday School Movement.

Then there were veteran Herbert Burrows, who for many years delivered the closing address at annual conferences; Clarion Vanners E. R. Hartley and Tom Kennedy; London Organiser E. C. Fairchild; black-bearded Jack Williams, leader of London's unemployed; John MacLean, already famous for his lectures on economics; Theodore Rothstein, expert on Chartism and foreign affairs; Jack Jones, silver-tongued orator from West Ham; Duncan Carmichael, Clapham Common speaker, afterwards Secretary of the London Trades Council; Zelda Kahan, persistent critic of Hyndman's "Big Navy" propaganda; and Dan Irving who in 1908 ran for Parliament in Manchester against Winston Churchill and Joynson-Hicks and was bitterly attacked for so doing by

H. G. Wells on the ground that he was splitting the Progressive (i.e. Churchill's) vote.

Members little known in those days but destined to become prominent later included Albert Inkpin, Joe Fineberg, Alf Watts, Pat Coates, Ernie Bevin (active in organising Bristol's unemployed) and Herbert Morrison.

The presence of the last-named in a militant socialist body may come as a surprise to those unacquainted with his early history. Contrary to a commonly held notion, Herbert was not an upper middle-class intellectual who entered the Labour movement in a patronising spirit bent on popularising the latest bourgeois economic theory. Actually he was, in his youth, an enthusiastic, almost fanatical student of Marx. The son of a policeman, he started life as a shop assistant with a passion for window-dressing (no doubt a great asset to his subsequent political career). In 1908 he joined the Lambeth Branch of the SDP.

True, his stay in the party was a short one as he left it the following year; but his reason for so doing was failure to convince his comrades of the correctness of Marxist political strategy as he saw it (and, what is more to the point, as most present day Marxists see it).

During his brief spell in the SDP young Herbert never tired of urging his fellow members to study the works of Marx and Engels and often walked about with the first volume of *Capital* tucked under his arm and the story goes that on seeing him approaching a comrade once remarked "Here comes the Class Struggle". Another habit of Herbert's at this time was to taunt his comrades with being "bourgeois" whenever they ventured to conform to social conventions such as wearing dress suits at dances.

Despite these affectations, Herbert's Marxism was not of a superficial character. On the contrary, he showed a comprehensive knowledge of the works of the two great thinkers such as could have been possessed by few men of his age at that period – as was demonstrated by his thoughtful expositions at open-air meetings and local debating groups of the theory of surplus value and the chapters in *Capital* dealing with "primitive accumulation". He took very seriously Marx's insistence on the closest possible contact between the advance guard of socialism and the organised workers and this led him to submit to his branch a motion to the effect that since the Labour Party had declared its independence of the bourgeois parties the SDP should join its ranks with a view to influencing its members in a socialist direction.

The motion met with a cold and hostile reception and was defeated by a large majority. The main arguments against it were that a genuine socialist party must preserve its independence and could not take orders from a body mainly composed of non-socialists. To which Morrison pertinently replied "You're not class-conscious but SDP-conscious".

Instead of pursuing his campaign inside the SDP, Morrison resigned his membership and joined the Brixton Branch of the ILP. He did so with the declared intention of undermining the influence of Ramsay MacDonald. For a time he acted up to this intention but eventually himself succumbed to MacDonald's influence, as we know too well, and by following in the footsteps of that arch apostle of reformism.

So much for the leading figures who were associated, for good or ill, with British social democracy 50 years ago. But what of the host of stalwarts who never entered the limelight, the local speakers, secretaries, chairmen and literature sellers who carried the branches on their shoulders? Faults most of them, in varying degrees, had in plenty; dogmatism and aggressiveness, contempt for sentiment for fear of being though unscientific, undue fondness for revolutionary phrases, somewhat childish affectations in dress (red ties, wide sombreros etc.) - but insincerity and unwillingness to make sacrifices were not among them. Such faults as they had were the faults of immaturity which time and experience would cure. It is certain that the stubbornness with which week after week and year after year, they hammered home the socialist gospel at street corners and dingy meeting places are bearing rich fruits today.

Mention has already been made of the "impossibilist" trend which existed within the SDF. This led, in the early years of the century, to numerous resignations and expulsions (in some cases involving whole branches). From these elements in the main sprang a number of tiny sectarian groups, each regarding itself as the only true Socialist Party and spending most of its time denouncing the larger bodies. The most vocal of these groups were the Socialist Party of Great Britain and the Socialist Labour Party.

The SPGB which, for some reason best known to itself, claimed to be superlatively Marxist, ruled out all "palliatives" (i.e. reforms within the capitalist system) and insisted that nothing short of complete socialism could be of any use to the working class. In spite of the undoubted ability of its leading propagandists, the SPGB membership remained microscopic, probably because its standards of socialist purity were so high that few could hope to qualify. The movement's general attitude towards this body was aptly summed up in Blatchford's quip "A Merry Christmas to the S.P.G.B. – all six of them".

The SLP, whose activities were mainly confined to Scotland, regarded all "politics" as deception of the workers and maintained that only Direct Action on the industrial field could establish socialism. This body also claimed to be Marxist and it must be admitted that the excellence and variety of its publications of the works of Marx and Engels were second to none. In later years a section of its membership adopted a more realistic attitude and played a worthy part in the formation of the Communist Party.

This sketch would be incomplete without some reference to the countless independent socialist organisations existing up and down the country on a district or professional basis (e.g. Hammersmith Socialist Society, Church Socialist League, Civil Service Socialist Society) to which must be added the vast army of the "unattached", viz., people holding socialist views without belonging to any organisation. Among the latter were many who were extremely active as "freelances". Perhaps the most famous of them was R. B. Cunningham-Graham, brilliant scholar and author who had suffered imprisonment during the '80s for his championship of the unemployed and liked to introduce himself as a descendant of "Bloody Graham of Cisiverhouse"

Finally there was Victor Grayson who, although nominally a member of the ILP, openly flouted its policy. A young man of 25, he made a meteoric appearance on the political stage in 1907 when, running as an independent socialist, he was elected MP for Colne Valley. True, he had received official Labour support, but it soon became clear that, in the eyes of the party pundits, this was far from justified. From the first his fiery eloquence made him a favourite on socialist platforms. The following year he was suspended from the House of Commons after protesting in defiance of the rules, against the government's failure to relieve the unemployed, at the same time denouncing the Labour Group as "traitors to their class". The gesture drew a tremendous response from all sections of the socialist rank and file and everywhere meetings addressed by him were packed to suffocation point. One such meeting held at Lambeth Baths enabled the local branch of the SDP to clear a debt to its District Committee – which had been accumulating for years. It need scarcely be added that no similar enthusiasm was displayed by the ILP leaders. Hardie and MacDonald denounced Grayson's action in no unmeasured terms while Philip Snowden remarked "I have never regretted anything so much in my life as helping that young man".

Such then was the nebulous collection of competing elements which, at the commencement of the present century, constituted Britain's socialist movement. Had it been possible to crystallise them into a unified and flexible force, the nation's history might have taken a different and, in the long run, less painful road.

2. A Changing Political Scene

Let us now examine the social and political background and the problems it posed for socialists in the years 1901-10.

The political scene during this decade was essentially a changing one, though the changes were not of an explosive character. Indeed, in comparison with the years 1911-20, it might well be regarded as a period of calm. But it was the calm before the storm. Moreover, the world-shaking events that followed were but the sequel to the impetus given to the forces beneath the surface of things which characterised the opening years of the century.

The second half of the nineteenth century had been a period of *relative* stability. True, there was little enough stability in the *individual* lives of most of the working class, constantly exposed as they were to the danger of losing what little they possessed. However, for good or evil, the social structure had the surface appearance of being fixed and settled and, apart from the scares over the Trafalgar Square "Riots" and the militant strikes of the unskilled labourers, no serious upheavals were threatened.

Craft unions bargained more or less amicably with employers able to bribe them with fragments of the fruits of colonial plunder. Liberalism and Toryism seemed to be established forever as the only possible alternative for British electors. The attitude of the general public towards "Women's Rights" was still one of tolerant amusement. Since the fifties this country had not been involved in a European war, such wars as did take place being waged against half-armed and more or less primitive peoples living a long way off. Hence there was little-anxiety regarding the imminence of any serious conflict involving the British people as a whole.

Such was the surface appearance of things. However, as all serious historical students are aware, in human society, least of all capitalist society, there is nothing static. Its laws of motion never cease to operate. And at the turn of the century, they had begun to operate with an increasing tempo.

The main features of this accelerated progress in the direction of an epoch of wars and revolutions, commencing in the second decade of the century are summarised below:–

Sharpening Unemployment Problem. The trade depression of 1903 and onwards brought with it a volume of unemployment and distress which provoked resistance that could no longer be appeased by the old methods – "Mansion House Funds" and such like "charitable" measures.

Rising Prices. Due, according to most economists, to an increase in the world supply of gold, prices of necessary commodities rose slowly but continuously during these years, thereby depressing the workers' real wages and providing the main objective basis for the biggest strike wave since 1889.

Twilight of Liberalism. The aftermath of the South African War, together with the revival of Protection by Joseph Chamberlain roused popular feeling against the Tory Government, with the result that it met with a smashing defeat at the end of 1905. Though the Liberals were returned with a record majority, the presence in a new Parliament of a compact group of Labour members owing no allegiance to either capitalist party signified the beginning of the end of Liberalism as a partner in the two-party system.

Women Suffrage. The long struggle for the franchise, led by the militant suffragettes, transformed the issue from one of academic discussion to one of immediate practical politics, thereby raising the level of women's political consciousness, which in the long run could not fail to develop the class-consciousness of working women.

The Drive to War. The final phase of imperialism had already commenced. No longer was Britain the workshop of the world. Germany had already outstripped her in industrial technique but lacked colonies of which Britain already had more than her "fair share". The balance could only be corrected by military means. Hence the armaments race. By 1910 the stage was set for war to re-divide the world among the imperialist powers. The only thing lacking was a convenient pretext.

Subsequent sections will deal in detail with the reactions to these developments of the various schools of British socialism and the social democrats in particular.

3. Rise of the Labour Party

Independent political action on the part of the organised workers of this country was not seriously considered until the late nineties of last century. Until then the nearest approach to it lay in occasional pressure upon one or other of the orthodox parties and the very rare adoption of working-class candidates for Parliament – usually of the Lib-Lab type (The only one who could reasonably claim to be independent was Keir Hardie).

It was the employers themselves (alarmed no doubt by the militancy of the dockers in 1889) who, acting through the legal profession, were responsible for a turn in the direction of working class politics. During the nineties it became a growing practice for employers to sue trade unions and their officials for damages in respect of losses arising out of strikes. This aroused some alarm among union leaders in consequence of which the Trade Union Congress of 1899 instructed its Parliamentary Committee "to invite the co-operation of Trade Unions, Co-operative Societies and other working class bodies in convening a Congress with a view to increasing the number of Labour members in the next Parliament".

Accordingly, a special congress was called at the Memorial Hall in February 1900. The response was disappointing. Only 129 delegates attended, representing considerably less than half the aggregate membership of the societies invited, viz.:

> Trade Unions   500,000
> ILP   13,000
> SDF   9,000
> Fabian Society 861
> [Note the absence of any co-operative societies]

Having agreed to set up a National Labour Representation Committee, the Congress proceeded to discuss its basis. The SDF took the initiative by proposing the following:–

> The representatives of the working-class in the House of Commons shall form there a distinct Party based upon the recognition of the class war and having for its ultimate object the socialisation of the means of production, distribution and exchange. The Party shall form its own policy for promoting practical legislation in the interests of Labour and shall be prepared to co-operate with any Party that will support such measures or will assist in opposing measures of an opposite character.

To this the ILP moved the following amendment:–

That this Congress is in favour of establishing a distinct Labour Group in Parliament who shall have their own Whips and agree upon their policy which must embrace a readiness to co-operate with any Party which, for the time being, may be engaged in promoting legislation in the direct interest of Labour and be equally ready to associate themselves with any Party in opposing measures having an opposite tendency.

The ILP amendment was carried by 53-39 (about one quarter of the delegates abstaining).

The first Secretary of the new body was James Ramsay MacDonald but this was largely a matter of mistaken identity, his name being confused by many delegates with that of James MacDonald, the popular Secretary of the London Trades Council.

At the "Khaki Election" which was held the same year, the Labour Representation Committee put forward 15 candidates, none of whom was successful.

Thus, the first venture of organised Labour in the political field was far from encouraging and it is possible that the new body would have died of inanimation but for the enormous fillip to its progress provided by the employing class in the shape of the Taff Vale decision.

The ruling of the Law Lords on this famous case is summed up by the Webbs as follows:–

A Trade Union, though not a Corporate body, could be sued in Corporate capacity for damages alleged to have been caused by action of its officers and injunctions could be issued against it and all its officers not merely from criminal acts but also from unlawfully though without the slightest criminality causing loss to other persons.

The decision cost the Amalgamated Society of Railway Servants approximately £50,000 including £23,000 in damages,

It was obvious that, if the situation created were allowed to stand, no union could support a strike without running the risk of bankruptcy. The only remedy was to change the law, which was a matter for Parliament.

This object lesson in the potency of political action was the one thing needed to rouse the union membership from its apathy. That the lesson was taken to heart is demonstrated by the fact that at the next LRC conference the numerical strength of the affiliated bodies doubled.

At this conference, held at Manchester, Harry Quelch, on behalf of the SDF, moved a resolution similar in terms to the one rejected at

Memorial Hall (committing the LRC to a socialist objective). This also was lost.

To the next Conference of the SDF the Executive Committee submitted a motion "That this Conference decides to withdraw from the Labour Representation Committee". Strongly supported by Quelch, it was carried by 54-14,

So British social democracy withdrew into the political wilderness where it remained for the next 12 years.

Quite a number of those who supported withdrawal at the time have since acknowledged that it was a tragic mistake. For instance, H. W. Lee says in Part 1 of *Social-Democracy in Britain* (written in the 1930s):–

> Looking back over events subsequent to the decision of the S.D.F. to withdraw from the L.R.C., I am now convinced and have been for a good many years that this decision was a sad mistake…
>
> As all members of the S.D.F. engaged in Trade Union work knew very well, Trade Unionists of all wage earners constituted the most favourable ground for Socialist propaganda. How many of those whom our propaganda and that of other Socialist bodies had weaned from the old notion of "no politics" in the Trade Unions but support for Liberal politicians outside, regarded our action as that of people who wouldn't play unless they got their own way? Events have since shown that we left the L.R.C. just when our Socialist views and policy would have been most invaluable inside the newly formed body destined in a very short while to become the Government of the country. All the propaganda that we did afterwards, all the influence we were able to bring to bear in a Socialist direction would have been very much greater indeed had we carried it on and exercised it as an integral part of the L.R.C. and not as an outside body at which many supporters of Independent Labour representation looked a trifle askance because of our withdrawal from the L.R.C. (pp. 159, 160)

Till the day of his death Harry Quelch never wearied in his opposition to any sinking of the identity of the SDF or its successor on a national scale in any non-socialist body. Yet, thanks largely to the efforts of men like himself, the isolation of social democrats from the mass of organised workers was far from being as complete as might appear at first sight. A well known figure at Labour conferences, both national and local, which he attended as delegate from his union, Quelch was anything but a silent critic and the same may be said of many other SDF stalwarts (e.g. Jack Jones, Will Atkinson, Fred Knee and Ben Tillett). Furthermore there was nothing to stop SDF branches from affiliating to local LRCs and trades councils, which, in fact, many of them did. As already mentioned, Will Thorne, who sat in Parliament as a Labour MP, was able in his election addresses to proclaim his personal socialist views in unmistakable terms. It is true, that, at the SDP conference of 1909, an ultra-left branch took the view that Thorne's position as a Labour MP was incompatible with his claim to be a social democrat and wanted the conference to call upon him to resign either his seat or his membership of the party – but the proposal received scant support from other delegates and none denounced this piece of "impossibilism" more emphatically than Quelch.

Following its second conference the LRC (which, in course of time came to be known as the Labour Party) made rapid progress. A number of seats were captured at by-elections between 1902 and 1906. In preparation for the General Election of December 1905, a canvass was made of all prospective candidates, to whom it was made clear that they would receive no support from Labour voters unless they pledged themselves to support the restoration of the pre-Taff Vale position as regards the legal status of trade unions.

At the election 50 Labour candidates were put forward, of whom no less than 29 were successful. Among the new-comers to the House were Ramsay MacDonald, Snowden and J. R. Clynes. In addition 12 working men, mainly miners, were elected under Liberal auspices. By 1910 most of them had joined the official Labour group.

The question of the legal position of the trade unions came up early in 1906 when the new Liberal government introduced a Bill much on the lines of the report of a Royal Commission set up by the late Tory government which recommended that unions should accept responsibility for their own actions, subject to certain amendments in the law. This raised a storm of protest, members rising from all parts of the House to explain that they were pledged to support the restoration of the complete immunity which the unions had been assumed to enjoy since the Trade Union Act of 1871. The effect of such unprecedented solidarity on the part of trade union electors was to compel the government, despite its huge majority, to pass the Trades Disputes Act 1906, which restored the legal position of the unions to what it had been prior to the Taff Vale case.

This initial success brought varied reactions from the members of the Parliamentary Group themselves and their trade union and socialist supporters (or critics). On the part of the Labour MPs, mainly orthodox trade unionists lacking any conscious socialist philosophy, there was a strong tendency to assume that, with the setting aside of the Taff Vale Judgement, their main purpose was accomplished and a separate party was no longer needed. This attitude was reflected among large sections of the trade union rank and file who were inclined to take the view that, now that the normal activities of the unions were re-legalised, a political party of their own was rather an expensive luxury.

On the other hand, the victory represented by the passing of the Trades Disputes Act could hardly fail to give encouragement to the socialist supporters of independent labour representation and in the ranks of the SDF there was a reaction in favour of re-affiliation.

Each year from 1903 onwards, efforts had been made to get the Labour Party to make a declaration in favour of socialism. At its 1905 Conference a resolution to that effect, moved by Will Atkinson of the Paper Stainers' Union was carried. Atkinson was under the impression that this automatically involved a corresponding amendment of the party constitution but was informed the following year that this was not the case, since the resolution in question was only an expression of opinion by the delegates. So at the Belfast Conference (1907) he moved a similar motion as an amendment to the constitution; but this was rejected by a 10 to 1 majority.

Nevertheless, a year later, the Hull Conference of the Labour Party carried the following resolution by 514,000 to 469,000:–

> That, in the opinion of this Conference, the time has arrived when the Labour Party should have as a definite object the socialisation of the means of production, distribution and exchange to be controlled by a Democratic State in the interests of the entire community and the complete emancipation of Labour from the domination of Capitalism and Landlordism with the establishment of social and economic equality between the sexes.

Again – an expression of the personal views of delegates. However, it is significant that the party objective as set out in this resolution was identical, word for word, with that of the SDP. Thus encouraged, the supporters of re-affiliation within the SDP again raised the question at their Manchester Conference held shortly afterwards. Three resolutions dealing with the subject were on the agenda. The main discussion took place on one from the Burnley Branch to the effect that in view of the resolution passed at Hull declaring Socialism to be the ultimate object of the Labour Party, the attitude of the SDF be reconsidered "provided it is made clear that all S.D.F. candidates run as Socialists".

On this occasion, Hyndman, who had strongly supported withdrawal in 1901, backed re-affiliation. Quelch, on the other hand, brought all his rugged eloquence to bear on securing its rejection; but this time his reasoning was decidedly below its usual level. This is illustrated by the following passage from his speech:–

If we pass either of these resolutions we shall be saying that we have been wrong for the last seven years and that we are going in sackcloth and ashes to confess it.

If true, why not? To our generation, accustomed to admit and correct political errors in the light of experience, this must seem strange logic coming from a man of Quelch's sterling qualities.

The Burnley resolution was defeated by 103 to 31 and the one for unqualified affiliation by 130 to 30.

Never again was Labour Party affiliation seriously discussed by the SDF (now SDP) until after it had been merged in the British Socialist Party.

Meanwhile, the enthusiasm roused by the quick passage of the Trades Disputes Act steadily subsided, although the ranks of the Labour MPs continued to be swollen as a result of by-election victories. (During 1907 Pete Curran was returned for Jarrow and Victor Grayson for Colne Valley),

Early in the next year Labour members made their one gesture of defiance to capitalism by introducing their "Right to Work" Bill which proposed to put all the unemployed to work, thereby depriving employers of the means of maintaining competition for wages, so that for the first time in history, the nation enjoyed the spectacle of Liberals and Tories trooping into one lobby in defiance of their joint interests. Unfortunately this was only a flash in the pan.

It was in the same year (1908) that, notwithstanding its non-socialist constitution, the British Labour Party successfully applied for membership of the International Socialist Bureau. Previously the British Section had consisted of representatives of our small socialist parties, constantly at loggerheads with each other and often, no doubt, a source of irritation and embarrassment to the leading members of the Bureau who, therefore, would be inclined to welcome the prospect of admitting a body possessing a membership more in conformity with continental standards. So the following motion, drawn up by Karl Kautsky, was submitted to the Bureau:–

> The International Bureau declares that it admits the English Labour Party to the International Congress because, without implicitly accepting the proletarian class struggle, it is practically engaged in that struggle; because, thanks to its own organisation, it is independent of the bourgeois Parties and places itself in consequence on the ground of International Socialism.

The manner in which representatives of British socialism reacted to this proposal is interesting.

Hyndman, sectarian leftist, urged the rejection of the application, since neither in theory nor in practice did the Labour Party accept the class struggle.

At the opposite extreme, Ramsay MacDonald, the super-opportunist took the view that, rather than accept the class struggle, he would prefer the Labour Party to remain where it was.

Bruce Glasier, whom we would describe as a centrist, was prepared to accept the motion as it stood.

Lenin, who was present on this occasion, welcomed the application but wished to amend the resolution to the effect that it should be regarded only as a first step towards a conscious class policy and a *socialist* Labour Party.

In the end admission was agreed to on the basis of Kautsky's motion.

It cannot be said that members of the Parliamentary Labour Party were unduly stimulated by their new dignity as fragments of International Socialism. On the contrary, they drifted along without any clear idea of where they wanted to go; and for nearly two years following the dramatic gesture of the "Right to Work" Bill, displayed little or no initiative – until at the end of 1909 the Osborne Judgement provided them once again with a definite and immediate purpose. Of this historic pronouncement, the Webbs write in their *History of Trade Unionism:–*

> What saved the Labour Party from decline and give it indeed fresh impetus in the Trade Union Movement was the renewed legal assault on Trade Unionism which, in 1909, culminated in the Osborne Judgment of the Highest Appeal Court by which the Trade Unions were prohibited from applying any of their funds to political activities and to the support of the Labour Party in particular.

What happened was that, in July 1908, a certain W. V. Osborne, a member of the Amalgamated Society of Railway Servants and an obvious stooge of the railway companies, took legal proceedings to restrain his union from spending any of its funds on political objects, contending that this was beyond its powers. Though this contention found little support in the legal profession, the case was carried through various courts right to the House of Lords which gave its ruling in favour of Mr. Osborne.

The fact that the railway bosses made such strenuous efforts to cripple independent political action by the workers (little as the "independence" had so far shown itself) speaks volumes for its *potential* value as a weapon of class struggle; while the extreme reluctance of successive Liberal governments to introduce legislation setting aside the Osborne Judgement showed an appreciation of the ultimate if not the immediate danger to their hold over the workers represented by the mere existence of a separate Labour Party in Parliament,

The two general elections held at the beginning and end of 1910 brought the Liberals back to power but in greatly reduced strength – so much so, in fact, that their continuance in office depended on the support of the minority Parties (Labour and Irish Nationalist). The Labour strength at this stage was 42.

So once again the Labour members had an object in life – to restore the freedom of the trade unions to use their funds for political purposes; but this time the fight was far more prolonged. No doubt, this is partly explained by the government's preoccupation with Home Rule and the House of Lords, but an additional factor was the extreme reluctance of the Labour group to endanger the Liberal majority. On at least one occasion they voted against their own amendment to a Bill rather than run the risk of bringing the Government down.

Undoubtedly the Webbs exaggerated when they wrote that "this challenge to organised Labour absorbed the whole interest of the Trade Union world for the next three or four years", for those were years of tremendous industrial struggles; but the statement is broadly true as far as the members of the Parliamentary Labour Party were concerned. At any rate nearly three years elapsed before the government, very unwillingly, passed the Trade Union Act of 1913 which, in the main, removed the crippling restrictions imposed by the Osborne Judgement. It gave powers to trade unions to include in their constitutions any lawful purpose so long as their main objects were covered by the Act of 1876. A novel feature was the institution of a "political levy" from which dissenting members could "contract out".

When, a few months later, World War 1 broke out, Labour was considered a sufficiently stable (and safe) factor in British politics to be invited to join a coalition government to "save civilisation from Prussian militarism".

4. The Suffrage Agitation

In the Victorian era it was customary to regard women either as dolls or drudges according to their social position. Working women in particular felt the full force of the double burden forced upon them by capitalism. As wage-earners or working housewives they shared the exploitation suffered by their menfolk; as women they experienced the mental and legal servitude common to the whole of their sex. The main features of the latter were unequal marriage and divorce laws, virtual exclusion from public life, professions and universities and a dual moral standard in matters of sex (men "sowed their wild oats" but women "went astray"). As is usual in the initial stages of revolt against any form of tyranny, this state of things was accepted without question by the vast majority and often defended with the utmost ferocity by the victims themselves. Thus, women tended to be the most ruthless critics both of their "erring" sisters and those of their sex who defied convention; while novelists of the type of Helen Mathers would wax lyrical over "woman's true sphere in life" and contrast "womanly" women with "Women's Rights" women, greatly to the detriment of the latter.

Fortunately, Helen Mathers was anything but typical of the leading women novelists of her time and it is refreshing to contrast her attitude with that of Sarah Grand who, in *The Heavenly Twins* ridicules the conventionally tolerant attitude towards male infidelities by making one of her characters, a wronged but submissive wife, remark "We lament and deplore but we forgive and endure."

Naturally the finer spirits, both men and women, bitterly resented a condition of things which placed one half of the nation in mental bondage to the other; and there can be no doubt that the efforts of such writers as William Morris, Bernard Shaw, Sarah Grand, Millicent Fawcett, Lydia Becker and the incomparable Olive Schreiner, besides effecting some improvements, did much to rouse the women of Britain to a sense of the injustice and indignity of their position. This was specially true of those women who moved in literary circles and those in touch with the early socialist movement.

Yet the fact remains that, at the turn of the century, "woman's sphere" was still the home (or the sweatshop) in the eye of the great majority and serious intellectual pursuits on the part of women continued to be frowned upon as "unladylike". "Advanced" women might reject the Victorian way of life but to the British public as a whole sex equality and votes for women in particular were just a joke.

Thanks, however, to the efforts of a group of determined women, it soon ceased to be a joke.

The National Union of Women's Suffrage Societies was already in existence and continued to agitate for the Parliamentary vote by the traditional orderly and respectable methods; but its agitation lacked vigour. The same could not be said of the Women's Social and Political Union, founded in 1903 by a number of ILP women, dissatisfied with the lukewarm attitude of their branch towards the suffrage question. Its driving force was Emmeline Pankhurst, widow of Dr. Pankhurst, well-known Manchester radical and friend of Ernest Jones and John Stuart Mill.

At first the WSPU conducted activities on other matters as well as the suffrage; but very soon these ceased and members concentrated their whole attention on "Votes for Women".

The turning point towards militancy came in May 1905 when, after months of lobbying and manoeuvring by WSPU members, a Mr. Bamford Slack was induced to put his name to a mild Bill granting a certain measure of enfranchisement to women.

Suffragists of all types from all over the country thronged the galleries and lobbies of the House only to hear their Bill received with roars of laughter and then "talked out".

It was the last straw. Nothing more was needed to convince the WSPU once and for all that the days of peaceful persuasion were ended and that the only way to get the claims of women seriously considered by Parliament, press and public was by making themselves a perpetual nuisance and plans were laid accordingly.

Thus, the *militant* suffrage movement was born. The first clash with the forces of "law and order" came in October of the same year at a meeting in the Free Trade Hall, Manchester, addressed by Sir Edward Grey (Foreign Minister in the 1906 Liberal government), Those involved in this opening engagement of what turned out to be a nine years war were Christabel Pankhurst (eldest daughter of Mrs. Emmeline Pankhurst) and Annie Kenney (a Manchester mill girl).

It happened that, a few weeks previously, a demonstration of Manchester unemployed had defied the authorities and caused a big traffic hold-up, with the result that within ten days, the Tory Government had passed a measure of unemployment relief. Two of the demonstrators had been arrested and this gave Christabel the idea that, by getting arrested herself, she could focus public attention on the suffrage question.

A request to the organisers of the Free Trade Hall meeting to receive a deputation was sent by the WSPU and ignored (as it was meant to be). So Christabel and Annie attended the meeting and when question time came, demanded to know whether a Liberal Government would give women the vote. The question was ignored by the platform. Advised by the Chief Constable, they sent up the question in writing but again no notice was taken. After shouting protests, the pair were hustled from the hall struggling all the time. In the course of the struggle, Christabel, with a view to being convicted of a technical assault, made a show of spitting in the face of a police inspector but not until they were outside the hall were they finally arrested.

Charged next day with spitting at the police inspector, Christabel was ordered to pay a fine of 10/- or go to prison for 7 days (in the third division). Annie Kenney was fined 5/- or 3 days. Both served their sentences.

Comments on the incident in the national press were much as might be expected, great horror being expressed that a young lady should so far forget the dignity of sex as to spit. Here are typical specimens:–

> If Miss Pankhurst desires to go to gaol rather than pay the money, let her go. Our only regret is that the discipline will be identical with that experienced by mature and sensible women and not that which falls to the lot of children in the nursery. (*Evening Standard*).

> If any argument were required against giving to ladies political status and power, it has been furnished in Manchester. (*Daily Mail*)

On the other hand, public opinion in Manchester itself was largely favourable to the two prisoners and a crowded meeting at the Free Trade Hall on October 20th gave them an almost unanimous welcome.

Early that December the Balfour government resigned and Sir Henry Campbell-Bannerman ("C-B") became Prime Minister. During the general election campaign that followed, members of the WSPU pursued a policy of persistent heckling at Liberal meetings, particularly those addressed by Cabinet ministers. The main purpose was to force these gentlemen to declare how they stood on the suffrage question which they were very reluctant to do as they wanted to talk about free trade, Chinese labour and other planks in the Liberal platform. In achieving this object the tactics partially succeeded – at least to the extent of obtaining from the Prime Minister a declaration that he personally was in favour of woman suffrage.

The chief sufferer from this policy of obstruction was Winston Churchill, at the threshold of his political career, who had recently transferred his allegiance from the Tory to the Liberal Party. As his constituency vas in Manchester, where the WSPU headquarters were situated he felt the full force of the onslaught. His first meeting at Cheetham Hall was in continuous uproar owing to the women's persistent demands that he should make his attitude clear. After a vain attempt to ignore the hecklers, Winston declared in his best John Bull style:

> Nothing could induce me to vote for giving women the franchise;
> I am not going to be henpecked into a question of such importance.

So the organised heckling continued throughout the whole campaign. Owing to Manchester's long association with the Pankhurst family, the audiences were generally sympathetic; so much so that indeed on the occasions when the interrupters were ejected, the greater part of the meeting came out with them, leaving Winston to talk to his bodyguard. As, however, election results are not decided by attendances at meetings, he won the seat, but by a smaller majority than those of the other Manchester Liberals.

In 1906 the WSPU commenced operations in London. On February 16th a crowded meeting at Caxton Hall, Westminster received the news that the King's Speech contained no reference to votes for women. Immediately platform and audience formed themselves into a deputation and marched through drizzling rain to the House of Commons where they were admitted in relays of 20, to lobby their MPs. When, on April 24th, a resolution to give women the vote moved by Keir Hardie appeared likely to be "talked out", women supporters in the gallery staged a demonstration of protest and were ejected with considerable violence by the police. On May 19th a large and representative deputation met the Prime Minister who expressed cordial agreement with the women's cause but added that, as some of his Cabinet were opposed, he could only preach the virtue of patience. "It would never do", he said, "for me to make a statement or pledge under these circumstances".

The reply of the WSPU, whose patience with promises had long been exhausted, was to intensify their anti-government policy and to devote special attention to their most outspoken opponent in the Cabinet, H. H. Asquith (who succeeded "C-B" as Prime Minister). Thirty women created a disturbance outside Asquith's house with the result that Annie Kenney and two others went to prison for six weeks rather than accept the alternative of being bound over for 12 months.

The public reaction to eight months of militant agitation by the suffragettes (by which designation they now came to be known) was on the whole hostile, True enough, their zeal and determination brought an enthusiastic response from a substantial minority of women (not to mention male) admirers who swelled the ranks as well as the funds of the WSPU during the early months of 1906, among the newcomers being many women of talent and influence and not a few of wealth. But it could scarcely be expected that the politically illiterate mass – the respectable poor, the gilded youth of suburbia, the readers of the yellow press – would take kindly to a campaign which so constantly forced their attention on a subject they did not want to think about. True to their varied types, such people were loud in their denunciations of the "disgraceful conduct" of the suffragettes and most prolific in their amiable suggestions as to how the offenders should be dealt with.

Yet it was astonishing how many critics who had given no thought to the subject before discovered that they supported the principle of woman suffrage but strongly objected to the tactics; this attitude being usually indicated in the smug phrase: "They are doing their own cause more harm than good".

It is probable that this hostility was not unexpected. The advance made consisted in the fact that the agitation had now reached a point at which woman suffrage was no longer regarded as funny. The backward sections of the public might dislike the tactics but could not ignore the issue.

Among the politically conscious minority a highly contentious question was the basis on which the claim for equal political status should be made. The slogan of the WSPU was "the franchise for women on the same terms as it is or may be granted to men" which, at that time meant in practice votes on a property qualification. This roused the suspicions of many sincere socialists, democrats and trade unionists who feared that the effect would be to strengthen the forces of reaction and were, therefore, unwilling to support anything short of complete adult suffrage. Certainly, there were grounds for their suspicions as quite a number of middle-class suffragists made no secret of their dislike of the prospect of giving votes to "every Tom, Dick and Harry" (and presumably Kate, Mary and Jane). On the other hand it is very doubtful whether this was the majority view in the WSPU whose founders were, after all, themselves ILP members; and it can be urged in their favour (1) that their chief concern was to find a formula which would lay the main emphasis on the removal of the sex disqualification and (2) they feared that a demand for adult suffrage would result only in manhood suffrage.

Had there been agreement on this point among the progressive sections of the population, the fight might not have been so bitter and prolonged. As it was, for better or for worse, the limited suffrage continued as the basis of the WSPU claims right up to 1914.

In the middle of 1906 what might be called the General Staff of the WSPU consisted of Mrs. Pankhurst and her daughters, Mrs. Despard, Mrs. How-Martyn and Teresa Billington (Joint Secretaries), Mrs. Pethick-Lawrence (Treasurer) Mary Gawthorpe and Mrs. Martel (Organisers), Elizabeth Robins, the novelist, Mrs. Cobden-Sanderson and Annie Kenney. They received valuable assistance from Mr. J. Pethick-Lawrence (afterwards a Labour Minister) both as speaker and organiser.

The next and, so far, the biggest clash with the authorities occurred in October when Parliament reassembled. A large deputation, which included the best known WSPU leaders, went to the House to demand a Woman's Suffrage Bill that session but were informed by the Chief Liberal Whip that the government were not prepared to introduce such a bill during their term of office. Immediately Mary Gawthorpe jumped on a seat and attempted to address the assembled lobbyists. When she was pulled down one woman after another followed suit until the whole deputation was ejected with the usual police violence, Mrs. Despard and Mrs. Pankhurst receiving specially rough treatment. Afterwards ten women, including Mrs. Cobden-Sanderson, Mrs. Pethick-Lawrence, Teresa Billington and Annie Kenney, were arrested. When the case was tried, Sylvia Pankhurst was also arrested, following a protest against her exclusion from the court.

The inclusion of the daughter of Richard Cobden among the offenders caused acute embarrassment to the government, especially when she offered to take full responsibility for the demonstration.

The ten received sentences of six weeks in the Second Division, with the option of being bound over for six months. Sylvia got 14 days in the Third Division. Later they were all transferred to the First Division. Sylvia served her full 14 days but the others were all released without serving more than half their sentences.

For over two years protests along these lines continued on an ever increasing scale, despite the elaborate precautions taken to exclude suffragettes from Cabinet ministers' meetings. On several occasions the House of Commons was stormed by huge deputations of women and most of the leaders of the WSPU – Mrs. Despard, Mrs. Drummond, Mrs. Pethick-Lawrence and Mrs. Pankhurst herself – took turns in gaol. During 1906-07 the total sentences served amounted to 191 weeks. This figure increased to 350 for the two following years.

In 1909 what may be termed the opening phase of the militant suffrage movement came to an end. So far the protests of the militants had been directed almost exclusively against the government, its ministers and its candidates. From 1909 onwards they took on new forms, involving ever widening circles. Limitations of space prevent us from following through all its subsequent stages, the bitter struggle that ended only with the declaration of war on Germany. Suffice to say that the forms of protest grew progressively more drastic – starting with window smashing and chainings to railings, proceeding to burning ballot papers, destroying property, damaging art treasures, arson and systematic interference with sporting events (in June 1913 Emily Wilding Davison died from injuries received after throwing herself in front of the King's horse at the Derby). Hardly a section of the public was unaffected by one or other of these activities.

The ethics and wisdom of such provocation of general hostility may be questioned; but not the fact that "votes for women" had become a living issue which none could disregard.

Naturally large sections of the public whose property, convenience or amusement was affected, were roused to fury and on many occasions the suffragettes felt the full force of the sadistic instincts of hooligan crowds (not to mention the police). Also, as the struggle became more bitter, the attitude of the authorities hardened and sentences grew in severity. At the same time the amazing courage, fortitude and tenacity of the women gained them ever more friends and admirers in progressive circles.

In the early stages of the suffrage agitation women prisoners accepted more or less passively their treatment as ordinary criminals. Now they demanded the status of *political* prisoners and, on this being refused, resorted to the tactic of the hunger strike (a form of protest not then familiar to the British public).

This confronted the authorities with a dilemma. Either they must give way, let the prisoners starve, or compel them to take food. The first hunger strikers succeeded in getting themselves released after prolonged periods of fasting (91 hours in the case of Mrs. Pankhurst). Then the Home Secretary decided on sterner measures. Unprepared to make martyrs of the strikers by allowing them to starve, he issued instructions to prison medical officers to feed them forcibly by means of a rubber tube passed through the mouth or nose into the stomach.

Judging by the medical evidence this was martyrdom enough. Here are some statements made at the time by distinguished medical authorities:–

> If anyone were to ask me to name the worst possible treatment for suicidal starvation, I should say unhesitatingly 'forcible feeding by means of the stomach pump'. (Dr. A. Moxey MD)

> This latest piece of official cruelty will quite possibly end in the insanity of some of the victims. (Dr. H. Roberts)

> As a medical man without any particular feelings for the cause of the suffragettes, I consider forcible feeding by the methods employed beyond common endurance. (Dr. Forbes Ross of Harley Street)

Dr. Forbes Winslow, an authority on the treatment of the insane, made a written statement to the effect that he had long discontinued the use of the stomach pump which he held to involve risk of injury to the heart and lungs and of sudden death in cases of mild heart disease.

A memorandum against forcible feeding signed by 116 physicians and surgeons was sent to the Prime Minister.

As soon as the news reached him, Keir Hardie tabled a Parliamentary Question. In his reply the spokesman of the Home Office described forcible feeding as "hospital treatment". Hardie retorted "A horrible beastly outrage" and Snowden cried "Russian barbarism".

Judging by the protests which poured in from all quarters, these sentiments were shared by millions throughout the country. They were admirably expressed in a cartoon which appeared in the organ of the WSPU depicting four of the world's worst tyrants (Abdul the Damned, Nicholas of Russia, Leopold of Belgium, and Alfonso of Spain) holding up their hands in horror at the spectacle of British women being forcibly fed under a "Liberal" government.

This state of things continued until the Spring of 1913 when the Government passed the Prisoners' Temporary Discharge for Ill-Health Act – better known as the "Cat and Mouse" Act. It provided for sick prisoners to be "licensed out" and taken back after recovery, the currency of their sentences being meanwhile suspended. In other words, a determined hunger striker sentenced to a few weeks might be in and out of gaol for years. Moreover, though the alleged purpose of the Act was to stop forcible feeding, this horrible practice in fact continued. Thus prisoners were faced with the twin horrors of forcible feeding and indefinite sentences.

Between July 1913 and June 1914 Mary Richardson, originally sentenced to three months for assaulting the police, was released and rearrested 9 times and forcibly fed three times (committing fresh offences during her "convalescent" periods). Mrs. Pankhurst, sentenced to three years in April 1913 was released and re-arrested 10 times.

This "cat and mouse" policy was still being operated at the beginning of August 1914.

Next to the heroism of the women the most noteworthy feature of the nine years agitation was the amazing efficiency with which the campaign was conducted. This applies not only to the direction of militant strategy but equally to such prosaic matters as office administration, money raising and publicity.

As regards finance, the following figures, showing the approximate annual income of the WSPU between 1908 and 1914 speak for themselves: –

1908-09	£20,000
1909-10	£32,000
1910-11	£29,000
1912-13	£28,500
1913-14	£37,000

On the publicity side it is only necessary to mention the huge and colourful processions and demonstrations organised by "General Drummond", in addition to countless thousands of meetings, ranging from mass gatherings at Albert Hall to small meetings in suburban streets and parks (in 1907-08 alone 5,000 were held). In its propaganda the WSPU enjoyed the assistance of many of the best known public figures in the country, including such Labour leaders as Keir Hardie, Philip Snowden and George Lansbury and such distinguished writers as Beatrice Harraden, Ciceley Hamilton, Laurence Houseman and George Bernard Shaw, But perhaps the biggest draw, apart from the leading suffragettes, was Israel Zangwill, the Jewish novelist, whose droll delivery and scintillating wit never failed to convulse an audience. A huge gathering at Queens Hall literally rocked with mirth when he remarked in his characteristic whimsical drawl that if the anti-suffragist view of life had always been accepted "Eve might as well have remained a rib".

As the fight grew in intensity Mrs. Pankhurst developed a Napoleonic complex and several times her dictatorial methods led to a split. The first occurred at the end of 1907 when Teresa Billington-Greig (as she had now become), Mrs. Despard, Mrs. How-Martyn and others left the WSPU to form the Women's Freedom League (which differed from the parent body only in its democratic constitution and slightly less drastic forms of militancy). In 1912 the Pethick-Lawrences resigned their membership owing to disagreement with the extreme tactics then adopted; and early in 1914 the East London section of the Union, led by Sylvia Pankhurst, whose membership was mainly proletarian, formed itself into the East London Federation of Suffragettes.

However, the great body of militant women remained with the WSPU which suspended its constitution after the secession of the Billington-Despard group. The members accepted this quite cheerfully, regarding themselves as soldiers on active service. But, while Mrs. Pankhurst might be the nominal dictator, the "power behind the throne", according to her sister Sylvia who ought to know, was Christabel, who henceforth worked out and directed the strategy of the movement.

Suffragettes were often accused of hysteria; but anything less hysterical than the generalship of Christabel is difficult to imagine. Allowing no touch of sentiment to stand in the way of political expediency, she pursued her objective with a singleness of purpose so cold-blooded and calculated as to be almost inhuman; brushing aside all issues save the one as of no account and, as both Keir Hardie and George Lansbury discovered, never hesitating to discard old friends and allies, once their usefulness had ended. As the years passed such socialist sympathies as she ever possessed fell to zero and her social outlook grew ever nearer to that of the Tories.

In the final stages of the campaign Christabel directed operations from Paris. For some months prior to the outbreak of war hopes were entertained of a compromise arrangement whereby militant tactics might be suspended in return for some sort of government pledge. To this end unofficial talks took place between Lloyd George, Sylvia Pankhurst and other suffrage supporters; but such concessions as Lloyd George was prepared to make were spurned by Christabel who announced from Paris that she would be satisfied with nothing less than a definite government pledge to enfranchise women in the near future.

Whether and, if so, how soon, victory would have been won, in the absence of war, it would be idle to speculate. There are, however, grounds for the belief that the government would have welcomed a pretext for giving way, provided they could do so without loss of face; and subsequent events seem to confirm this view.

On the outbreak of hostilities, Mrs. Pankhurst and Christabel lost no time in offering the services of their organisation in defence of the democracy which they had declared for so long to be non-existent. The offer was accepted and was quickly followed by a general amnesty for the imprisoned militants. For three years the former leaders of the suffrage agitation did their utmost to outdo Northcliffe and Bottomley in the violence of their jingoism, thus providing the government with plausible grounds for passing the Act of 1917 "in recognition of women's war services". This Act was neither adult suffrage nor the limited measure formerly demanded but extended the Parliamentary franchise to (1) women over 30 who were occupiers or wives of occupiers of land or premises of not less than £5 annual value and (2) women over 30 holding university degrees. Illogical as it was, it represented the first big breach in the sex barrier which was the point at issue. So the fight was won – at the expense of international solidarity.

Mrs. Pankhurst and Christabel ended their days as diehard Tories. So did "General" Drummond who continued to exercise her organising abilities – in the interests of the employing class. Shortly before the miners' lock-out in 1926 she organised a procession headed by a banner bearing the words "Miners Demand District Agreements" (the exact reverse of what the Miners' Federation was actually doing).

On the other hand Sylvia Pankhurst opposed the imperialist war throughout and became the leading figure in an East London socialist group which linked up with the Communist Party in 1921. Mrs. Despard also continued to serve progressive causes until her death when over 90.

It only remains to summarise briefly the effects of the impact of the suffrage crusade on the various sections of the Labour and socialist movement.

In the early stages the WSPU, ILP and Labour Party were so closely linked that the suffragists were regarded almost as a branch of the political Labour movement. However, this state of things could not last in view of the rigid line adopted later by the WSPU leaders. For the latter had no use for any party unless it was either in a position to deliver the goods or prepared to subordinate every other issue to that of a limited women's franchise; and in neither case could either of these conditions be fulfilled. Inevitably, therefore, the two movements drifted steadily apart.

The first serious rift came at the Belfast Labour Congress (1907) to which Woolwich Trades Council had submitted a resolution for the extension of the franchise to women on the same conditions as to men. Harry Quelch moved an amendment declaring that "any measure to extend the franchise on a property qualification is a retrograde step and should be opposed". The amendment was carried by 605,000 to 268,000. In face of such an emphatic vote none of the Labour MPs were prepared to sponsor a Women's Enfranchisement Bill on a limited basis.

Relations continued to worsen until they reached a point, where, because of their reluctance to embarrass the government, the Labour chiefs received much the same treatment from the suffragettes as Cabinet ministers. Keir Hardie and George Lansbury were the foremost champions of the WSPU standpoint within the Parliamentary Labour Group. In 1912 Lansbury took the line that his party should oppose the government on all questions until it brought in a measure for women's suffrage. Finding himself in a small minority, he went so far as to resign his seat in Parliament and sought re-election as an independent suffrage candidate. Unfortunately, WSPU members and Lansbury's local supporters found it impossible to work in harmony, with the result that the seat was lost by 731 votes. This quixotic gesture, though popular with the rank-and-file, met with scant appreciation from the stern realists who led the WSPU.

When the "Cat and Mouse" Act was passed, 14 Labour members voted for it and 7 against. An amendment moved by Keir Hardie declining to strengthen the law against hunger strikers until the government had redeemed its pledge to carry through its final stages any votes for women measure, which a free vote of the House had accepted on second reading, received only 4 votes.

Relations with the ILP as a body followed much the same course, except that the break came a little later. It is true that the Derby Conference (1907) carried by a large majority a resolution similar to the one defeated at Belfast shortly before but for some reason which has never been made clear, Mrs. Pankhurst and her followers in the ILP withdrew without warning a little later. Ramsay MacDonald who never liked either the WSPU or its leaders did his best to widen the breach.

From time to time the Women's Co-operative Guilds took part in suffrage demonstrations, but always those of a constitutional character.

Robert Blatchford and the *Clarion* were on the whole sympathetic to the militants – mainly because of their pluck.

The old *Daily Herald* alternated between wild enthusiasm for the suffrage cause – as when George Lansbury made his stand in 1912 – and equally strong support of the "rebels" against the dictatorial methods of the Pankhursts.

The one important section of British Socialism which at no time made any pretence of sympathy with the demands of the militant suffragists was the SDP. Long committed to complete adult suffrage, its membership, with a few exceptions, was solidly against any limited measure, E. Belfort Bax, Herbert Burrows, Hyndman and Quelch being specially critical of what they called the "Fine Lady Franchise".

While some leading suffragettes were being tried for incitement, Will Thorne (the party's one MP) told a meeting of the unemployed in Trafalgar Square that instead of rushing the House of Commons they should rush the bakers' shops – following which he was ordered to be bound over or go to prison for six months. As he chose to be bound over while the women chose prison, his gesture fell rather flat.

Even forcible feeding failed to rouse any sympathy in the columns of *Justice*, whose attitude was summed up in a cartoon depicting two hungry tramps, one of whom said to the other "*We* don't want forcible feeding, Bill".

The following factors may help to explain, if not to justify, the attitude of dour hostility maintained by social democrats towards this long and bitter campaign:–

> (1) The emphasis placed by many suffrage speakers on their rights as "women who pay rates and taxes" (instead of as human beings).
> (2) The constant flow of cash from wealthy donors into the coffers of the WSPU.
> (3) The fear of clerical influence over women voters.

(4) The indifference of the suffragettes to the furtherance of any cause but their own (especially in regard to strikers and unemployed workers).

Undoubtedly, these were powerful considerations which, taking the short view, may well have appeared overwhelming. Yet, in the long run, it is probable that they were more than offset by the stimulus to political thought and activity among women which resulted from the removal of the sex barrier.

Ernest Belfort Bax (1854-1926). SDF theoretician and ardent anti-feminist.

5. The Fight for the Unemployed

Though, prior to 1914, unemployment in Britain never reached the dimensions of the '20s and '30s, it had long been sufficiently constant and widespread to demand increasing government attention and was the subject of frequent legislation during the early years of the present century.

At that time it was impossible, in the absence of anything approaching complete official statistics, to ascertain the precise volume of unemployment which existed at any given time. The main sources of information on the subject were the returns published by trade unions granting unemployment benefits to their members, which only covered a fraction of the organised workers and these, on the whole, the most highly skilled.

The following table, compiled from information supplied by all unions making returns and quoted by William (now Lord) Beveridge shows their unemployment rates for the years 1901-08:–

1901	3.3%
1902	4.0%
1904	6.0%
1905	5.0%
1906	3.6%
1907	3.7%
1908	7.8%

(The corresponding figures for the years 1894-1900 were much lower.)

These figures reflect the depressions of 1903-05 and 1907-09 to addition to the "normal" margin of unemployment necessary to maintain wages at an "economic" level from the profit-making point of view.

For the victims of this chronic social disease not fortunate enough to belong to benefit societies, the only relief available at the commencement of the century was from "charitable" sources; failing which able-bodied unemployed, unable to maintain themselves were dealt with as paupers in accordance with the infamous "principle of less eligibility" which laid it down that their situation "shall not be made ... as eligible as the situation of the independent labourer of the lowest class".

Naturally, the growing numbers of unemployed, as well as of those workers enlightened enough to realise the threat to their own standards of hordes of hungry men clamouring for jobs, were not prepared to tolerate this position indefinitely. Hence, the increasing frequency during the period under review of demands by organised groups of unemployed under socialist inspiration for the provision of work outside the degrading conditions of the Poor Law. As usual, government action followed in the wake of agitation, in proportion to the degree of pressure exerted.

The first serious attempt, by capitalist standards, to tackle the problem by legislation was the Unemployed Workmen Act of 1905 which was passed shortly after the Manchester riots already referred to.

This Act set up local distress committees, the principal functions of which were to get to know the conditions of labour in their respective areas and assist distressed cases by emigration, removal to other areas or provision of temporary work (which would not involve loss of civil rights).

Expenditure from the local rates was limited to ½d. in the £ (or 1d. with the consent of the Local Government Board). This was supplemented by an Exchequer grant in 1906.

The number of distress committees formed when the Act came into force was 89 in the provinces and 29 in London. In the latter case there was also a co-ordinating body, known as the Central (Unemployed) Body for London. No committees were set up in Scotland until 1907 and then only 14.

The number of cases relieved (including dependents) in England and Wales during 1905-06 was approximately 311,000 and the figures for the two following years showed a substantial reduction.

Usually the employment provided was of a socially useful but unprofitable nature, e.g. road making and repairing, sewerage construction, street cleansing, laying out recreation grounds. In a number of cases "unemployed colonies" were established. The best known of these was the Hollesley Bay Farm Colony run by the Central (Unemployed) Body for London.

Article V of the Act laid it down that men employed on such schemes should be paid less than would be earned by an independent labourer. In other words, the "principle of less eligibility" still operated.

In the first three years of their existence distress committees assisted the emigration to Canada of 3,386 heads of families and 10,000 dependents. The Act also gave distress committees powers to establish labour or employment exchanges covering most of the London area was set up in 1906.

Thus, the 1905 Act, while it may have had some effect in allaying the prevalent discontent, made no progress whatever towards the solution of the real problem – how usefully to employ the total labour force of the nation (how, indeed, could any capitalist government be expected to do so?)

Just before going out of office the Tory government which passed this Act appointed the famous Royal Commission on the Poor Laws and Relief of Distress, whose terms of reference were to inquire into and make recommendations to improve (1) the working of the laws relating to the relief of poor persons in the United Kingdom, and (2) the various means which have been adopted outside of the Poor Laws for meeting distress arising from want of employment, particularly during periods of severe industrial depression.

After sitting for over three years the Commissioners produced two lengthy reports of which the Minority Report, signed by Mrs. Sidney Webb, George Lansbury and two others aroused far more public interest than that of the majority. The main difference between the two reports concerned their attitude towards the old Poor Law. As regards unemployment, their recommendations were substantially the same, viz.:–

(1) A national system of labour exchanges
(2) Education and training of the young for industrial life
(3) Regularisation of employment (i.e. the use of public employment to steady the demand for labour)
(4) Unemployment insurance

It will be observed that three of these proposals concerned either the relief of distress arising from unemployment or the filling of available jobs. Only (3) envisaged an actual increase in the total volume of employment. Needless to say, it was never acted upon during the period between the issue of the Commission's reports and the outbreak of the First World War.

An Act passed in September 1909 authorised the Board of Trade to establish and maintain labour exchanges wherever they thought fit; also to assist exchanges maintained by other authorities, to take over such exchanges and to make general regulations for their management. The term "labour exchange" for purposes of the Act was defined as "any office or place used for the purpose of collecting and furnishing information either by keeping registers or otherwise respecting employers who desire to engage work-people and work-people who seek engagement or employment".

The Board proceeded to set up as speedily as possible a national system of exchanges under their own control. Existing exchanges, which they considered to be running efficiently (including those of the Central London Body) were taken over and the rest closed down. At the end of 1910, 148 exchanges were open. Two years later this number had risen to 414, the number of vacancies filled reaching 828,000.

Compulsory insurance against unemployment made its first appearance in this country as Part II of the National Insurance Act 1911. Unlike Part I of the Act which covered health insurance it was not general but was restricted to the following trades: building, construction of works, shipbuilding, mechanical engineering, construction of vehicles and sawmilling carried on in connection with any other insured trade or of a kind commonly so carried on.

The card and stamp system was introduced under this Act. As regards unemployment, the weekly contributions of employer, worker and government were 2½d., 2½d. and 1d., respectively. Unemployment benefit was 7/- per week up to a maximum of 15 weeks in a year and subject to numerous provisos and disqualifications.

Behind all this elaborate legislation it is not difficult to recognise the strategy of a ruling class determined to maintain its hold over the general body of wage earners. Confronted with the unwillingness of growing numbers of both actual and potential unemployed to submit to the inhuman conditions imposed under the Poor Law, capitalist politicians were prepared to retreat from their former *laissez-faire* attitude to the problem to the extent of making the lot of the unemployed slightly more tolerable; but always their efforts were directed towards relieving the distress arising from the unemployment rather than removing the causes of such distress. As for the very limited number of public works schemes set up, the authorities always insisted that the conditions of the "unemployed" engaged upon them should be "less eligible" than those of men doing similar work under private enterprise.

For it was vital to the capitalists that the gap between the standards of the profit-producing workers and the "reserve army" should be as wide as possible. With characteristic cunning, they and their henchmen justified this by appeals to the snobbery of the politically backward workers whose "sturdy independence" was contrasted with the shiftlessness and indolence of the victims of unemployment (conveniently ignoring the fact that, in the absence of such a gap the bargaining power of the employed would be enormously increased).

While the object of capitalist policy was to maintain the widest possible gap between the living standards of employed and unemployed, class-conscious workers realised that their interests lay in precisely the opposite direction – i.e. in reducing the gap to a minimum. Hence, the agitations carried on during this period with the object of providing the unemployed with useful work under the most favourable conditions.

In these agitations a leading part was played by the social democrats who, in the years of depression, organised and led large sections of the unemployed in a nationwide effort to wring concessions from the ruling class. Needless to say the SDP membership had no illusions regarding the prospects of solving the unemployment problem within the limits of the capitalist system; but this did not prevent them from appreciating the undermining effects upon that system of any substantial easing of the competition for wages that would enable workers in private employment to make increasing demands upon their exploiters. (In those days, it must be remembered, no elaborate machinery existed for preventing and postponing strikes; nor did TU leaders advocate a wage-freeze).

Agitation along these lines was, of course, nothing new for the SDF. As far back as 1886 social democrats had led a huge procession of unemployed through the West End of London where the taunts of wealthy residents provoked the demonstrators into smashing the windows of the fashionable clubs – thereby causing such panic that the Mansion House Fund (for relieving the unemployed) jumped in a few days from under £3,000 to over £39,000.

This was the highest point reached in the first phase of the unemployed agitation which died down in the late '90s. The depression which started in the winter of 1902-03 was the occasion for a revival of activity. Some idea of the progress of the agitation and the problems encountered during the next seven years can be gathered from the following passages extracted from SDF publications:–

In conjunction with the London Central Council of the S.D.F. we carried on an agitation among the unemployed during the winter months. A difficulty was felt in how to make the unemployed show themselves to the public. The difficulty was solved to some extent, by the organisation of daily parades during which collections were made, the collections being afterwards shared among those who marched in the processions. The making of collections was not a method which any of us cared to adopt! Still, while the parades and collections were still under our control, they certainly impressed the public with the fact that a great and growing number of people were out of employment. Experience, however, has taught us that this method of parading the unemployed can only be carried on for a few weeks. Small groups of men whose cupidity may have been excited at the prospect of a greater share in the collections if they broke off from the main processions, soon reduced the business to a farce. The agitation was concluded by a mass meeting in Trafalgar Square. The agitation, while it lasted, undoubtedly assisted the unemployed in many districts in obtaining work from the Local Authorities, while it caused many Committees to spring into existence for the theoretical discussion of the unemployed problem and for the practical alleviation of the distress. The S.D.F. were represented on the National Unemployment Committee which held its conference at the Guildhall on February 27th and 28th. (Executive Committee Report to 1903 Conference).

The growth of unemployment in the country has brought the question of the unemployed prominently to the front and we took the initiative, on the suggestion of our Organisation Committee, in pressing for a Special Autumn Session of Parliament to legislate upon the unemployment problem. Owing both to persistent Socialist agitation and the increasing number of Socialist and Labour members on various local bodies, the unemployment question received far more attention from Local Authorities than was the case years ago. But the more steps taken locally to deal with this glaring evil in capitalist society, the more it is proved that the question is a national and not a local one. Our demand for a Special Autumn Session of Parliament was taken up, we are glad to say, by a large number of prominent public people as well as by local bodies in all parts of the Kingdom. We make special reference to the fact that this demand was originated by the S.D.F. for it was so quickly taken up by others that the S.D.F. – as usual – received little recognition for its initiative in this direction...

Boards of Guardians, Town and Borough Councils have been circularised by the S.D.F. setting forth our old proposals, advocating also a Special Autumn Session of Parliament and later, demanding that the promise of the Unemployment Bill made in the King's Speech should not be disregarded by the Government. M.Ps., members of the Cabinet and public men generally have been written to either from the Central Office or by Branch Secretaries. In this connection, we think it only right to place on record our recognition of the great amount of work done by many Branch Secretaries who have spared neither time nor trouble in sending out a mass of correspondence to public bodies, public men and the Press with the result that the Organisation has been brought into considerable public prominence.
(EC Report to 1905 Conference)

Our Unemployed Agitation ... has been continued as far as means permitted but has been hampered by our limited pecuniary resources. We co-operated with the L.R.C. in the demonstration in Hyde Park on the Unemployed and we have sent representatives to various conferences on the question. Towards last autumn the matter again came to the front for, though the returns of the Trade Unions showed a somewhat decreased proportion of their members unemployed, the number out of work especially among the so-called unskilled workers was still very great. Members of the S.D.F. took an active and vigorous part in unemployed agitations and meetings and in London the S.D.F. joined with the London Trades Council in the Central Workers' Unemployed Committee which co-operated in the women's deputation to Mr. Balfour on November 6th and organised the remarkable procession of the Unemployed through the West End of London on November 20th. The feeble reply of Mr. Balfour to the Women's Deputation, together with the declarations of Mr. John Morley and Lord Rosebery ... that they had no remedy for the unemployed problem furnished us with excellent opportunities for Socialist propaganda. Mr. Joseph Chamberlain in his Bristol speech, having stated that the only manner for dealing with the unemployed problem was that proposed by Tariff Reform, the S.D.F. challenged the Ex-Colonial Secretary to discuss publicly his proposals with a member of the Organisation, but the challenge was declined.

Last Autumn, in accordance with the instructions given, a communication was sent to the National Administrative Council of the I.L.P. recommending the establishment of a joint committee for carrying on a vigorous Socialist agitation on the question of the Unemployed. The reply urged co-operation with the L.R.C. Permission was granted our comrade Harry Quelch to join the "Right to Work Committee" – a Committee of Socialists and others who have taken an active part in the Unemployed Movement – as it was thought advisable that a member of the S.D.F. should be upon that Committee, though every member is there in his or her private and not representative capacity. A manifesto on the Unemployed was issued in December and about 100,000 copies were distributed.
(EC Report to 1906 Conference)

Several great meetings of Unemployed have been held ... a "Right to Work" National Council of prominent Socialists has been formed ... the Unemployed grabbed land at Manchester, Bradford and West Ham.
(*Socialist Annual*, – edited by Th. Rothstein – 1907)

J. E. Williams organised a successful march of the Unemployed through London on the date of the opening of Parliament – February 1907; also held meetings at Tower Hill with Will Thorne, J. O'Grady and others.
(EC Report to 1907 Conference)

Meetings on the Unemployed Question were held by Jack Williams on Tower Hill, three times a week all through the year.
(*Socialist Annual* 1908)

A march of unemployed ex-service men was organised on December 23rd, the day on which the 'Daily Telegraph' gave a dinner at the

Albert Hall to the veterans of the Indian Mutiny. The object of the march was to point out that many ex-soldiers and sailors were starving and could not wait for 50 years in order that they might then be regaled with a sumptuous repast.

We have given considerable attention to the question of the Unemployed. It was felt last year that the increasing depression in trade would make the position of the mass of the working classes of this country even more terrible than it was in 1885-7. Consequently, we felt it necessary that the S.D.P. should be the first in endeavouring to organise a serious agitation on behalf of the Unemployed so as to bring as much pressure as possible to bear upon the Government to take up the question on a national basis. Branch Secretaries, were, therefore, asked to reply to enquiries sent out as to the state of trade and the numbers out of work; what action should be taken by the S.D.P. locally; and whether such action should be carried out in conjunction with other organisations. We regret that the inquiries did not elicit sufficient replies from our Branches to enable us to initiate a simultaneous agitation throughout the country on behalf of the Unemployed.

The London section of the E.C. appointed a small committee specially to deal with the question of the unemployed who in turn appointed Comrade J. E. Williams as Chief Organiser of the Unemployed in London. The main object of the agitation was to create, if possible, a feeling among the Unemployed that they must put themselves in evidence on every possible occasion. Meetings and marches were organised in London and reported in the Press, so that it became generally recognised that the movements of the unemployed were the result of our work. Delegates from the London Committee of the S.D.P. attended a meeting called by the National Right-to-Work Council for the establishment of a special Council in London and E. C. Fairchild was appointed Secretary to that Council; and other members of the Party have been engaged on active work on the agitation in connection with our Unemployed Committee. We concluded the agitation in the Metropolis with a great demonstration of the Unemployed workers to the West End Squares on February 14th and co-operated with the Right-to-Work Council in organising the Women's Demonstration on February 15th, the day of the opening of Parliament.

Out of the earlier unemployed demonstrations arose the prosecution of Will Thorne M.P. for the speech delivered on October 10th and for which he was bound over in sureties for 12 months. Another important incident in the unemployed agitation was the action of Victor Grayson, M.P., in the House of Commons. On two occasions he prevented the business of Parliament being carried on

until he was excluded and then suspended from the House of Commons, in order that the question of the unemployed should be brought prominently to the front, protesting against the Licensing Bill taking precedence of this infinitely more important question. The general agitation on behalf of the unemployed and the criticisms to which their inaction subjected them seemed for a time to have had a wholesome effect on the Labour Party, for its members certainly exhibited a much bolder front on the question of the Unemployed at the beginning of the present session than they did before; but since then nothing further has been done by them.
(EC Report to 1909 Conference)

At Glasgow on more than one occasion the out-of-works woke the City Fathers to some little sense of their responsibility. In the Metropolis the London and District Right-to-Work Council and the Social Democrats arranged some very effective marches to the West End. Some unemployed 'At Homes' were held in several of the Squares in successive weeks one of which was violently broken up by the police; a special march took place on the day prior to the opening of Parliament; and on the opening day itself a great march of women and children took place from Cavendish Square to the Horticultural Hall from whence deputations were sent to the House of Commons.
(*Socialist Annual* 1910)

This year a movement took place among unemployed ex-soldiers, due largely to a few of our comrades who collected the names and addresses of ex-service men out of work. A march to Trafalgar Square and a deputation to Mr. Haldane were arranged for Saturday, October 30th. The march of trained men headed by a special banner looked very different from the ordinary processions of unemployed and caused considerable public attention. Mr. Haldane received the deputation, our comrade (Ex-Sergt. Major) Edmondson, acted as spokesman and the War Minister was heckled in a manner that he did not expect when he consented to receive the deputation.
(EC Report to 1910 Conference)

After 1909 the agitation slackened off. There were several reasons for this. First, unemployment in the years preceding the First World War was somewhat less acute. Further, the attention of social democrats was largely taken up with the formation of the new British Socialist Party and the problems it brought in its train. Most of all, as far as the workers were concerned, the situation was dominated by the great industrial struggles of 1910-14.

The activities described above were in the main organised directly by the Executive Committee, usually in the Central London districts. The picture would, therefore, be far from complete without some reference to the many vigorous agitations carried on both in provincial towns and the outlaying areas of London.

Mention has already been made of the effect of the militancy of the Manchester Unemployed Movement in speeding the passage of the Unemployed Workmen Act of 1905.

The same year witnessed the historic "Hunger March" of the workless makers of army boots from Raunds. With them came a contingent of unemployed workers from Northampton, led by James Gribble – a local stalwart who later became an SDF councillor. He was the leading figure in a very strong agitation in Northampton, in the course of which the unemployed surrounded the headquarters of the local Board of Guardians and scared the latter into granting their demands – road and park improvements; boots and clothing for the workless etc.

A year or two later the Bristol Socialist Society (affiliated to the SDF) carried on a strenuous fight on behalf of the local unemployed. Following the lead of the National EC they set up a Right-to-Work Committee whose Secretary was no less a person than Ernest Bevin. This Committee opened a Bread Fund as a result of which 3545 loaves were distributed to unemployed families on Christmas Eve. However, the most effective as well as most dramatic stroke of the campaign was the visit of the organised unemployed to Bristol Cathedral. This episode and its results are vividly described by Francis Williams in his biography of Ernest Bevin.

> One Sunday shortly before morning service in Bristol Cathedral a great crowd of unemployed assembled in the Horsefair. There they formed in orderly procession and, with Bevin at their head, marched to the Cathedral. As the service began they entered and, with Bevin leading them, silently took up places along every aisle of the great Church. They remained there without stirring throughout the service, many of them clearly in great distress from hunger, all of them poorly clad; a mute challenge to the Christian conscience of every worshipper. When the service ended they filed slowly and quietly out of the Cathedral and without speaking a word, reformed into procession and marched back to the Horsefair. There, after a few words from Bevin, who told them to go back to their homes without disturbance, they dispersed.
>
> The manner no less than the purpose of this demonstration aroused immediate public sympathy. Prominent Church groups

headed by the Dean waited upon the City Council to demand, in the name of the Christian community, that some action should be taken at once to relieve unemployment in the City. Faced by this strong expression of public uneasiness, the City Council at last agreed to meet Bevin's Committee. Thereupon, he proposed that the City Council should approach the Local Government Board and ask for a grant to relieve local unemployment by public works including the building of a lake in one of the chief parks in the City. After some debate the Council accepted as practical the schemes put forward by Bevin and his Committee and agreed to approach the Board. The grant was approved and work was found for a large number of men at wages not much below those ruling in normal employment.

Other towns where organised struggles of groups of workless took place under socialist leadership were Glasgow, Bradford and West Ham.

In addition were the hundreds of contests for seats on local councils and Boards of Guardians at which the proposals of the social democrats regarding unemployment were brought prominently to the front. (The first item in the SDF Municipal Programme was "The organisation of Unemployed Labour upon useful work").

There is ample evidence in the columns of the local press for the years 1905-10 that the directives of the SDF leadership in this respect were seriously followed up by the branches situated in the South London suburbs. This applies in particular to the six large Boroughs of Southwark, Bermondsey, Camberwell, Lambeth, Wandsworth and Battersea – as indicated by the frequent references in the *South London Press* and *South Western Star* to the activities of the local social democrats, usually in co-operation with other socialist bodies and/or trades councils, in mobilising the unemployed for action to bring pressure to bear on the authorities to adopt measures of relief. A noteworthy feature of these agitations, whether or not they were officially sponsored by broader bodies, was the high proportion of cases in which the leading role was played by members of the SDF.

Of the above-mentioned boroughs, the one hardest hit by unemployment was Bermondsey, where, at the end of 1907, the proportion of registered unemployed to population was quoted by the Distress Committee as 11.6 per 1,000 – well above the corresponding figures for the other five boroughs.

The resulting distress was specially acute during the winters of 1907-08 and 1908-09. To make matters worse, the Finance Committee of the LCC refused to find £3,600 recommended by the Parks Committee to enlarge the artificial lake in Southwark Park. This aroused the anger of the organised workers of the borough who formed a Park Lake Extension Committee which held meetings of protest.

As an instance of the haphazard methods adopted to relieve distress, cards were issued to 400-500 men entitling them to work at snow clearing whenever a fall should occur. All that was lacking was the snow.

In January of 1908 no less than 12 members of the Bermondsey SDP waited on the Guardians to demand action regarding both unemployment relief and school feeding. Their spokesman was J. V. Wills who stated that 10% of Bermondsey workers were unemployed and complained that local labour was not being employed on the extension works at the infirmary as agreed. Pointing out that, of 1,583 necessitous children the Borough, only 412 had been fed, he urged the Guardians to press the LCC to put in force the Education (Provision of Meals) Act 1906.

The Guardians agreed to urge the LCC to put the Act into force without delay and referred to a committee the questioned local employment at the infirmary.

The acute distress continued throughout the following winter. In October the Right-to-Work Committee (with Wills as Chairman) held large public meetings at Rotherhithe and Bermondsey Town Halls which passed resolutions urging the LCC, Borough Council and Guardians "to exercise the powers vested in them to mitigate the suffering rising from Unemployment by putting in hand at once all available work". The meetings appointed comrade Wills to lead a deputation to the borough council where he complained of delay, produced figures and submitted proposals. For half an hour, following his statement, councillors bombarded him with questions dealing with all aspects of the unemployment problem. "It was", reported the *South London Press*, "really a debate with rhetorical cutting, parrying and slashing".

Refusing to leave the building until they received a definite reply to their proposals, the deputation were finally informed that the committees had been instructed to hold special meetings to consider them.

Early the next year, following further deputations and some stormy scenes in the town hall gallery, the council resolved, subject to their Finance Committee submitting an estimate, to raise a loan of £5,000 for paving streets.

An equally vigorous fight, in which social democrats played a prominent part, was waged in the adjoining Borough of Southwark. Here is a passage from the *South London Press*, dated January 1908:–

> A deputation of Southwark workers and residents, representing local branches of 37 trade unions, waited on the Borough Council to impress upon them the need of at once starting as much

remunerative work as possible in order to relieve the enormous amount of distress existing in the Borough; also to ask the Council to memorialise the Government to deal with unemployment as a national problem and to press on the Local Government Board to remove obnoxious clauses in application forms for unemployed workers which debar unemployed from obtaining work if they have received parish relief in the previous 12 months.

In this case also the spokesman was a well known SDPer – R. C. Morrison (later a Co-operative MP and finally a Labour Peer) He said that 10-40% of workers in the trades enumerated were out of employment and that there had been 601 more applications to the Guardians for outdoor relief during the previous fortnight than in the corresponding period of the previous year.

The council agreed to approach the government to deal with the question as a national one and to apply to the LCC for a contribution to public works.

In October of the same year a Mr. Jackie led a deputation to the town hall and warned the council that "if they did not deal with the Unemployed the Unemployed would deal with them". He then voiced a demand that was frequently made at this period – that the council exercise their powers to establish Municipal Workshops under the Act of 43 Elizabeth.

A week later R. C. Morrison was again the leader of a deputation – this time to the Guardians, whom he warned that if any violence occurred the authorities would be responsible.

Following this pressure a number of concessions were obtained, viz. drainage works to employ 300 men were agreed upon; the council accepted by 23-23 a recommendation from their Finance and Works Committee to consider levying a 1d. rate to provide work for the Unemployed; and works involving an expenditure of £7,340 were accepted, subject to the cost of labour being met by the Central Unemployed Body.

A similar state of affairs existed in Camberwell where, at the end of 1907, the Guardians informed the borough council that the workhouses were full and any big increase in the number of applications for poor relief would involve enormous cost to the ratepayers.

Agitation on behalf of the workless in this borough was very widespread but suffered from the weakness that it was directed from several centres. Engaged in it were, in addition to the local SDP, the Camberwell Unemployed Committee, the Camberwell Socialist Council and the Right-to-Work Committee of the Dulwich ILP. Had the activities of these bodies been better co-ordinated, they would probably have accomplished more. Still, their joint efforts certainly kept the authorities on their toes for 18 months.

For the whole of the period from the autumn of 1907 to the spring of 1909, excepting the summer months, both Guardians and borough council continued to receive deputations from all quarters, often accompanied by disturbances in the gallery. (On one occasion four separate deputations addressed the council). The proposals put forward were many and varied, ranging from dairy farming to the establishment of Municipal Workshops under the Act of 43 Elizabeth.

Two SDP stalwarts who came into prominence in connection with these activities were Lockwood and Tom Quelch (son of Harry). Between them they led at least 6 deputations, Lockwood stating the case for the Camberwell Socialist Council.

A feature of the situation in this borough was the way in which council and Guardians continually pressed each other to take action. When, at long last, they reached the point of holding a joint meeting to discuss measures of relief, the only conclusion to which their collective wisdom could arrive was that "the question of unemployment and the remedy for same can be adequately dealt with only by the Imperial Government".

The one positive decision by the council of which there is any record was one to undertake channelling works at a cost of £2,560 and sewerage works at a cost of £719.

The former Wandsworth Board of Guardians held jurisdiction over a territory roughly comprising the areas of the present Boroughs of Wandsworth and Battersea. Hence we find the unemployed of both areas taking common action as described in the following news item of more than 50 years ago:–

> On Sunday afternoon about 200 of the unemployed of Battersea and Wandsworth marched to Trafalgar Square where ... a meeting was held. Several of the speakers criticised severely the actions of the Wandsworth Guardians who had given them stones when they asked for bread. "Joe" Chamberlain came in for some nasty knocks, being described as the "British Butcher" and told that bread was already dear enough without any one trying to make it dearer. Mrs. Despard, a Guardian, was one of those who braved the icy winds which swept round the plinth of the Nelson Column and made an energetic speech. After an hour and a half of talk a resolution of extended dimensions was put and carried, one thing asked being that Parliament should set apart a special day for discussing the question of the unemployed. (*South London Press*, 21.1.05.)

The reference to "stones when they asked for bread" relates to the institution of stone-breaking which was then considered a suitable occupation for an able-bodied pauper. In this connection, another item from the same paper is worth quoting:–

> In the parishes comprising the Wandsworth Union viz. Battersea, Clapham, Wandsworth, Putney, Streatham and Tooting, no fewer than 1,100 persons had lost their Parliamentary votes owing to their having been obliged to seek Poor Law Relief, the majority through accepting work at the Union stoneyard during the distress of last winter. (*South London Press*, 23.9.05.)

A week later appears a report of a demonstration on Clapham Common, organised by the local ILP, which carried a resolution calling on the government to arrange an Autumn Session to amend the Unemployment Act. It was moved by Jim Connell (Author of the "Red Flag"), seconded by Dora Montefiore (SDF) and supported by J. Keir Hardie,

From then onwards, there is very little record of further activity in the Wandsworth part of the Union area, beyond a meek request from the trades council to the borough council to open the libraries at 7 a.m. to enable the unemployed to consult the newspapers in the hope of finding jobs. It received a characteristic reply to the effect that the "Situations Vacant" columns of various papers were on the notice boards outside the libraries between 7 and 7.30.

On the other hand, the Battersea end of the area was the scene of some stirring events. In November 1905 the borough council received 5 members of the Battersea Workmen's Committee, led by Duncan Carmichael, who stressed the need to find work for the large number of unemployed in the Borough.

A month later, a towns meeting, called to discuss the new Unemployed Workmen's Act, appointed a deputation to interview the Guardians. Its spokesman was W. H. Humphreys (SDF candidate for the LCC) who urged the board to make full use of their powers under the Act. Afterwards a mass meeting addressed by Humphreys and Carmichael, was held outside the Guardians' premises.

However, little action appears to have been taken by the authorities at this stage. Distress was less acute during the winter of 1906-07 but a serious situation developed the following autumn. This was reflected in the columns of the *South Western Star* – an extremely reactionary local weekly – which commented nervously on the "bands of men congregating on Battersea streets" and later expressed alarm that for the first time the prevalent distress was seriously affecting the skilled trades.

Deputations were again the order of the day. First came one from the local branch of the Amalgamated Union of Carpenters and Joiners whose leader informed the council that "the oldest member could not recollect such a period of depression as now". It was followed, a week or two later by a larger deputation, representative of both skilled and unskilled workers, with Duncan Carmichael again the chief spokesman (his fourth turn in that capacity).

The meeting held on this occasion was an historic one in the annals of Battersea and is reported at length in the *South Western Star* of 29.11.07. First, Carmichael drew attention to the high proportion of unemployed among the organised workers – carpenters 15%, bricklayers and stonemasons 30%, labourers 35-40%. He was followed by another member of the deputation who dealt specially with the unskilled workers. Most of the councillors were evidently impressed with the gravity of the situation and convinced that it called for drastic action. After a long discussion they resolved by 31-16 to raise an additional sum of £25,000 for works of unemployment relief before 30.9.08 and referred the matter to their Finance Committee to make the necessary arrangements "at the earliest possible moment". A special meeting of the council held the following week, adopted a recommendation of the Finance Committee to raise a Supplemental General Rate of 3d.

This brought into action the Battersea Municipal Alliance (an organisation dedicated to the ratepayers' pockets) who denounced the rate as illegal and, supported by the local Tories and the *South Western Star*, immediately set on foot a campaign to reverse the council's decision. Their first step was an attempt to get the magistrate to refuse to sign the rate – usually a pure formality. Failing in this, they arranged for one of their members to lodge an appeal against it at Newington Sessions House. In March, 1908, judgment was given in favour of the appellant. In other words, the rate was quashed with costs against the council, on grounds that only a legal expert could understand.

Naturally, Battersea's Tories were all cock-a-hoop and the successful appellant became a Nine Days Hero; but, fortunately for the men who secured jobs, the works had already started. The council met their immediate difficulty by raising a bank overdraft of £25,000.

The unemployed returned to the charge in October when Carmichael and Humphreys led yet another deputation to the council. Both indulged in some very straight speaking, making it clear that the unemployed were in no mood to be put off with any scare talk about the rates. Carmichael submitted lists of streets in urgent need of repair, together with other necessary public works covering four sheets of foolscap.

Thus stimulated, the council prepared a scheme of road improvements and other public works, estimated to cost £16,298 for submission to the Central Unemployed Body.

In Lambeth also, the socialist and labour movement had a long record of activity on behalf of the unemployed, which extended from the beginning of 1905 to the middle of 1909.

The *South London Press* for 21.1.05 published the following resolution passed by the Lambeth and District Trades Council to which the local SDF was affiliated:–

> The Lambeth and District Trades & Labour Council requests the Lambeth Borough Council to immediately apply for a loan of £10,000 from the L.G.B. to be used for the purpose of providing useful work for the unemployed of Lambeth during the present distress. There is much public work of an urgent and necessary character which requires to be done in Lambeth, viz., the repairing, pointing and polishing of the woodwork in the interiors of public buildings, repainting and pointing the exteriors, the overhauling of vans etc., the overhauling of all machinery under the control of the Borough Council, the cleansing and sweeping of roads etc. Further, that an 8 hour day or 48 hour week (or less) with a full 24 hours rest once a week be immediately instituted by the Lambeth Borough Council to be applied to the whole of the Departments under their control, thereby benefiting those employed by relieving them of overwork and the unemployed of the District through the employment of more labour.

Shortly after this, the same paper reported a meeting at Princes Hall, Kennington Road, organised by the trades council and attended by 800-900 people. W. Lock (Gasworkers) presided and W. Wright (Cabmen's Union) moved a resolution condemning stone-breaking, declaring the unemployed problem to be a national one and proclaiming socialism as the only final remedy. (Will Wright was an old social democrat who, earlier, worked with William Morris, rejoining the SDF after the collapse of the Socialist League.)

A copy of a resolution in somewhat whimsical terms, passed by the Lambeth [Branch of the SDF appeared in the *South London Press*, dated 27.1.06:–

> That this Branch of the S.D.F. greatly regrets that the Lambeth Borough Council should have disgraced itself in the eyes of Lambeth working men by refusing to receive a deputation from the unemployed of the Borough on Thursday, January 18th. It trusts that this fact will not be forgotten at the elections next November and

also draws the perfectly fair inference that the Council has done so little for the unemployed that it is afraid to face their representatives.

The increasing distress of the winter of 1907-08 led to a protest by Councillor Iremonger (the first Labour man to sit on the Lambeth Council) who, at the December meeting protested that, out of 750 registered unemployed work had been found for only 42. He also complained of the refusal of the officials to allow the use of the baths for a public meeting.

Evidently the latter point was conceded, for in January a well attended and enthusiastic conference on unemployment and underfed school children was held in the board room at Lambeth Baths, under the auspices of the Trades Council, both ILP and SDP branches being represented. The speakers were Mrs. Snowden, Will Thorne, Pete Curran, Frank Smith, George Lansbury and Herbert Burrows, with Councillor Iremonger in the chair.

Despite this feast of eloquence, not to mention the local activities carried on since 1905, there is no evidence of any serious action having been taken by the authorities until the end of 1908. This must be attributed, at least in part, to the very vigorous autumn campaign led by the local SDP. So energetically were the Lambeth unemployed mobilised for action that at one period the branch was making batches of recruits every week.

The leading spirit of the campaign was Fred Boyd, a young man of 23 who emigrated to America two years later. Twice within a fortnight he led deputations to the council from the organised unemployed. On the first occasion he presented a memorial from the Lambeth Trades Council, in which it was suggested that working hours of council employees should be reduced to 48 a week with no decrease in wages; proceeding to demand (1) that the Act of 43 Elizabeth be put in force (2) that a Towns Meeting be called to discuss the plight of Lambeth's 8,000 workless and (3) that the council press for extended powers under the Unemployed Workmen Act. On his second visit he repeated his demand for a Towns Meeting and persisted in talking after his official time had expired until his voice was drowned by cries of "Chair".

Later, when the unemployed went to interview the Guardians, they took advantage of this incident to refuse to recognise Boyd as spokesman. His place was taken by Wyatt, another SDPer, but at a subsequent visit he also created a scene and the deputation was ejected by the police.

At the end of the year the Guardians made a minor concession regarding the method of paying men engaged at the labour yard, while the council resolved to undertake relief works, costing £6,531, subject to the usual contribution from the Central Unemployed Body.

In the early months of 1909 there were further protests both by the organised unemployed and by local Labour leaders, especially when the labour yard was closed; but agitation along these lines gradually died down. Then the SDP decided to approach the problem from another angle – that of housing. A committee was appointed to inquire into conditions in the working class streets of North Lambeth. As might be expected their investigations disclosed an appalling state of affairs. The bulk of the work was actually done by one man, F. Newbury, who covered many streets with house-to-house visits and compiled a mass of information, involving altogether 75 cases of defective housing.

The following letter, dated 6.5.09, was then sent to the borough council:–

Sir,

On behalf of the Lambeth Branch of the S.D.P., certain members were appointed to undertake the visitation of workmen's homes in this Borough. On April 29th the houses mentioned in the enclosed report were visited and the information here given was collected by the undersigned.

The Lambeth Branch of the S.D.P. wishes to lay stress upon the extent of the work that could be provided by the Borough council if the Sanitary Laws and Public Health Acts -were administered without reference to private interests. Unemployment, which still causes grave distress, might thereby be greatly relieved in the Borough and at the same time, the public health be guarded and improved.

The facts here given have been known to exist by all good citizens for many years past and the enclosed report is now presented in the hope that the Borough Council may become equally cognisant of the infamous conditions in which great numbers of the working class in Lambeth are living, to the danger of all the residents in the Borough.

The S.D.P. definitely charges the Lambeth Borough Council with administering the Sanitary Laws and Public Health Acts in the interests of private property to the detriment of the public health and tenders the evidence here given in support of that charge.

We are, sir, yours faithfully,

M. F. Boyd. Hon. Sec.

F. Newbury. Organiser.

The following are a few cases taken from the report which accompanied the letter and relate to houses all in one street:–

Rain comes through ceilings; walls in bad condition; stairs broken; over-run with rats.

Tenant lived here 50 years; has seen Sanitary Inspector twice in that time; stairs broken; rain comes through roof; back room, broken wall.

Tenant lived here 4 years and has not seen Sanitary Inspector; ceiling and walls in very bad condition; 5 papers on wall; verminous; paint dirty; staircase and dust-bin defective; kitchen door broken; top rooms in exceptionally bad state.

Ceilings, wall and floor in bad condition; tenant lived here 5 years; landlord done nothing by way of repairs in that time; ceilings and walls broken; floor upstairs repaired with wood from an orange box.

Tenant lived here 11 years; all repairs in that time done by himself; 3 years ago wife fell downstairs through the dangerous condition of the stairs.

Kitchen ceiling and wall in bad condition; stairs dangerous, giving way beneath the weight of a person on them; lodger recently fell down and since that time the stairs have been patched with two pieces of wood; hand rails missing; Sanitary Inspector unseen for 3 years.

Pipe broken through floor of front room; filth oozing through flooring; rain comes through the roof; ceiling, walls, paper, stairs, need repair or cleansing; defective dustbin.

It appears to be a matter of comment among the residents in ------ Street that the Sanitary Inspector is not seen until after illness has broken out.

Both letter and extracts were published in the *South London Press*, causing quite a sensation and provoking a lively correspondence. In due course particulars of all the 75 cases were submitted for the council's consideration.

When the council met, on June 17th, to discuss the complaints, there was time for little else on the agenda. Officials and councillors waxed indignant over the "outrageous charges", denied the least concern with private interests, abused the branch, sneered at the "amateur inspectors", blamed the neglect of the tenants and disclaimed responsibility for some of the worst cases; but had to admit that it had been found necessary to serve notices in respect of 29 out of the 75 dwellings listed.

One lone voice was raised on behalf of the tenants and the party – that of Councillor Iremonger who confirmed Newbury's statements from his own observations, adding, "Despite the misrepresentation to which they had been subjected, the SDP had not moved in vain".

Thus, in five big South London boroughs out of six investigated, we find evidence of sustained efforts by SDP branches to rally the victims of unemployment for struggle; nor is there any reason to doubt that these campaigns were equalled in intensity by the branches covering the working class areas North of the Thames. All of which serves to demonstrate that London's social democrats 50 years ago were by no means as isolationist as they are often painted and were far indeed from confining their activities to the preaching of socialist abstractions. The value of their work cannot be measured solely by the immediate concrete results achieved – which admittedly fell far short of the objectives aimed at – but equally, if not more so, by such intangible factors as the experience gained and passed on to the generation of militants who led the wider struggles of the unemployed between the wars.

6. The SDF in Action

The three opening years of the century were, for the SDF, years of continuous internal conflict, the annual conferences of 1901-03 being largely occupied with bitter feuds, resulting in hosts of resignations and expulsions, in some cases of entire branches. The main controversial issues involved were (1) the correct attitude of social-democracy towards Parliament and (2) the legitimacy or otherwise of supporting palliative measures, short of the complete abolition of capitalism. There were two breakaway movements – one, very much under the influence of the American anti-parliamentarian Daniel De Leon, which, in 1903, formed the Scottish Socialist Labour Party, the other, most numerous in London, which rejected all palliatives and founded the Socialist Party of Great Britain (1904).

Despite a considerable temporary loss of membership, there can be no question about the benefits which the SDF derived from the shedding of these elements. Comparatively free from disruptive influences (though the "impossibilist" trend still persisted in a less aggressive form) it was in a position to turn its attention outwards and proclaim its message with a vigour and unanimity that had not been possible for some years past. Hence, the period of 1905-09 may well be regarded as one of the most productive in the history of the organisation, both as regards the quality of its socialist propaganda and the strength of its agitation for immediate demands.

The following may be taken as a fair summary of the SDF line at this stage:–

Socialism. Systematic propaganda, by platform and pamphlet, explaining the class struggle and the need for socialism and exposing the evils of capitalism.

Parliament. The election of a socialist group to the House of Commons, which would use Parliament mainly as a platform for agitation and exposure. (In the absence of such a group, it was never possible to put this to the test).

Partial Demands. Mobilisation of the workers to force concessions from the ruling class, successful fights for such concessions being regarded as stepping stones.

It is with these fights for partial demands that we are mainly concerned here.

The seven year struggle to win concessions for the unemployed has already been described in some detail.

Next in importance came the movement for the state feeding of school children, in which the SDF, both nationally and locally, was actively engaged for several years. This was a big bone of contention between the SDF majority and the section of "impossibilists" who founded the SPGB.

The latter used to argue "What is the use of feeding school children? It will only make them better wage slaves."

To which the stock reply was: "Yes, but it will also make them better socialists." And the more sympathetic might well add: "In any case, how can we refuse to feed school children?"

Now that the experience of several successful revolutions has convincingly discredited it in practice, such a line of opposition in principle to all palliative measures may seem incredible to militant socialists. Yet, half a century ago when there had been no breach in the world capitalist front, this distortion of the theory of "increasing misery" was not without a certain plausibility. (After all it only differs in degree from the standpoint of present-day pseudo-militants who argue: "Wait till the slump comes." "The workers are too well off." "They'll learn through their stomachs.")

However, plausible or not, the SDF as a whole did not hold this view but, on the contrary, fought strenuously for immediate improvements in the workers' conditions, and not least for school feeding.

Actually for tactical reasons, the demand was put forward for the full state maintenance of school children, but the aspect of it which won wide public support was school feeding.

The case for state maintenance was admirably stated by Rose Jarvis, a leading member from Croydon, in the *Socialist Annual* for 1906. Below are some extracts from her article:–

> The S.D.F. has for many years agitated for the 'State Maintenance of Children' and has pointed out that it is the duty of the State to look after those who are irresponsible and unable to protect themselves. Under present conditions specially – owing to lack of employment, uncertainty of work, short time and low wages – it is quite impossible for a man to provide the necessaries of life for his little ones.
>
> The State pretends to educate the children. To do this efficiently the physical condition must first be considered and a thoroughly healthy body established... To attempt to educate starving and ill-clad children is not only a crime but a waste of energy and public money. The community should, therefore, see that the recipients of instruction are properly nourished and clothed and housed under healthy conditions...

To-day the expenses of the Army and Navy, the Civil Service, National Education and other things are met out of the national exchequer and this maintenance of the children could be provided in the same way...

Whether we regard the matter from the point of view of economy, justice or humanity, there is no valid objection to State Maintenance.

The main campaign conducted by the SDF on this issue was launched in April 1904, in pursuance of a decision reached at that year's Annual Conference. The "SDF Notes" in the issue of *Justice* for 30.4.04 included the following:–

> In accordance with instructions received from the Annual Conference, the E.C. are arranging for a campaign in favour of the Free Maintenance of Children in our Public Schools... a series of meetings will be organised in London on Sundays, May 15, 22 and 29... There will be similar activity in the Provinces.

How effectively their plans were carried into effect in the course of the year that followed may be gathered from these passages, taken from the Executive Committee's Report to the 1905 Conference:–

> We congratulate the members of the S.D.F. on the splendid success which has attended our efforts in regard to the agitation for the most important of our palliative proposals – that of State Maintenance for the Children in our Public Schools... A number of important meetings upon the subject were held in various parts of the country, including a series of open-air meetings in London, which led up to a demonstration in Trafalgar Square on Sunday, August 28th, in which a number of Metropolitan Trade Unions took part. Since the reopening of Trafalgar Square for public meetings, under police regulation in 1892, meetings in that famous spot have never been equal to what they were previous to its being closed in 1887; but the meeting in favour of State Maintenance was unquestionably by far the greatest gathering that has been held there since meetings were again permitted. In addition to meetings, correspondence has been conducted between branches and their local M.P.s pretty well throughout the year ... and considerable prominence given to the question and to the activity of the S.D.F. in connection therewith. Special leaflets on the subject have been issued by the S.D.F., one containing a diagram setting forth the various diseases arising from underfeeding and the Twentieth Century Press have produced a penny pamphlet written by our comrade J. Hunter Watts.
>
> But above and beyond all was the National Labour Conference on State Maintenance held in the Guildhall, London, on January

20th, 1905. This Conference, suggested by the S.D.F., received the support of the Trades Union Congress Parliamentary Committee and the London Trades Council and a Joint Conference Committee was responsible for the arrangements. It was most gratifying surprise to the S.D.F. delegates to find that the resolution pledging the Conference to the full principle of State Maintenance was passed with such an overwhelming majority by the 250 delegates who were present.

...Take the two questions which we have made practically our own – State Maintenance of Children and the Unemployed. The public attention which has been devoted to these two questions during the last six or eight months is due almost wholly to our efforts... Starting with the free feeding of children which was denounced as one of the most hopeless proposals that any band of dreamers could possibly have put forward, we have gone on to State Maintenance and nothing shows the necessity of going for full measures in this land of compromise more than the fact that the advocacy of State Maintenance has brought us within measurable distance of State Feeding – the recognition that the nation as well as the parent is responsible for the upbringing of children.

It is true state feeding was not long delayed; but it was "state feeding" of a most grudging kind, hedged in with restrictions and reservations. The next year witnessed the passing of the Education (Provision of Meals) Act. It enabled Local Education Authorities, if they thought fit, to feed necessitous children and recover the cost from the parents; but if they wished to provide free meals it was necessary to adopt Section 3 of the Act. Moreover annual expenditure on school meals was limited to the produce of ½d. rate. As might be expected most education authorities, being under reactionary control, displayed no initiative in the matter.

Needless to say, there was small jubilation in socialist ranks at the passing of this measure. The most that could be said for it was that it represented the "thin edge of the wedge" (and a *very* thin one) as far as school feeding was concerned. Nevertheless, it did provide an obvious basis for further agitation. Clearly, the next step was to press for the adoption of Section 3 of the Act in as many areas as possible; and this, in fact, was the line pursued.

Among the many education authorities which made no effort to use their powers was the London County Council; which was not at all surprising, in view of its composition. When the Act was passed (in December 1906) the Progressive majority on that body was nearing the end of its term of office and was probably too pre-occupied with its prospects of getting back to take on any new responsibilities. They were, in fact, swept from power the following spring by the Municipal

Reformers, after a campaign conducted on the best Tammany Hall lines, in which the former council majority were widely denounced as "wastrels" and lavish use made of a poster portraying a sly spiv informing the London electorate "It's your money we want". It was not to be expected that a bunch, elected on the basis of appeals to such sentiments would favourably consider any expenditure out of the rates on a purpose so unremunerative as the feeding of hungry children. So the immediate prospects of getting the Act operated in London were anything but encouraging.

In these circumstances, the SDF leadership decided to devote special attention to the campaign in London and at the 1908 Conference were able to report:–

> In conjunction with our London Committee we have carried on a most strenuous agitation in London to endeavour to force the L.C.C. to put in operation Section 3 of the Education (Provision of Meals) Act 1906. We felt it was of considerable importance that no effort should be spared on this attempt, for if the L.C.C. could have been forced to take this step, their example would probably have been followed by many other cities and towns. A crowded and enthusiastic meeting in support of this demand was held in the Queen's Hall on Wednesday, January 15th; a petition was organised by the London Committee and over 21,000 signatures obtained on a bleak Saturday afternoon; and a deputation waited upon the Education Committee of the L.C.C. to urge that the Council should pay attention to the resolution of the Queen's Hall Meeting and the petition submitted. The Education Committee, however, declined to receive the deputation. In addition to the foregoing, many Public and Towns meetings have been organised throughout London on this matter and resolutions carried demanding that the Government should make the Act compulsory, remove the limit of the halfpenny to the rate to be imposed and make a grant from the Imperial Exchequer towards the cost of providing food under the Act.

Among the London Boroughs where the demand received active support from the branches were Lambeth, Bermondsey and Southwark.

Reference has already been made to the fact that the operation of the Act of 1906 was one of the demands put forward at a mass meeting held at Lambeth Baths in February 1908, which was supported by all sections of the local labour and socialist movement.

In Bermondsey, towards the end of 1907, the SDP, Trades Council, Labour Protection League and London Carmen's Trade Union all sent letters urging the borough council to use its influence with the LCC to secure the adoption of Section 3 of the Act. This led to a long debate in the course of which several councillors supported an approach to the LCC. Typical of the opposition outlook is a speech by a Councillor Dumphreys who said that when he was on the London School Board, voluntary aid supplied all the necessities of the children, adding that "it was often found that boots provided were taken from the feet of children and pawned". Not surprisingly, this provoked uproar in the gallery, accompanied by shouts of "Liar".

Later Bermondsey social democrats deputised the Guardians in force and succeeded in persuading the Board to urge the LCC to put the Act into operation without delay.

At Southwark, about the same time, in response to pressure from the trades council, two Towns Meetings were held to discuss school feeding at opposite ends of the borough – one at Lavington Street Baths, the other at Newington Public Hall. Both were reported at some length in the *South London Press*. At each meeting the case for school feeding was stated by J. G. Webster (a member of the SDP Executive) and the opposition view by a Southwark councillor named Attenborough. In the case of the Lavington Street meeting the councillor, who met with a very hostile reception, managed to get in first with a resolution to the effect that "provision of meals can be amply met by voluntary effort and that the action of the Mayor in appealing for voluntary contributions for provision of meals be approved". To this Webster moved the following amendment: "That Section 3 of the Act be put into operation by the LCC forthwith and that the representatives of Southwark take active steps to give effect to the resolution; that the Act be amended to make its operation compulsory and that only by full State Maintenance can the best development of the children be secured."

According to the *South London Press* the amendment was carried by an overwhelming majority, only about a dozen voting against. At the Newington Hall Meeting the procedure was the same, except that Webster's motion was taken as the resolution and Attenborough's as the amendment. On this occasion the only opposition to school feeding came from the mover and seconder of the amendment. The meeting closed with the singing of the "Red Flag".

It would be gratifying to be able to add that the agitation was successful in forcing the LCC to give way; but, unfortunately, this does not appear to have been the case as the subject is not mentioned in subsequent Annual Reports.

Other domestic issues on which action was taken nationally by the SDF during the period 1901-10 were education; exposure of the sweating schemes of the Salvation and Church Armies; and democratic reform – with special reference to adult suffrage. But none of these campaigns could compare either in length or intensity with those dealing with unemployment and school feeding. In the case of adult suffrage, it must be confessed that the efforts of the social democrats were put quite in the shade by the more concentrated and single-minded agitation of the Suffragettes.

A national campaign of a different kind was that conducted in opposition to Haldane's Territorial Scheme.[2]

The SDF was never a pacifist body. On the other hand, it was equally opposed both to conscription and a small professional army, supplemented by a part time territorial force (one of its objections to the latter was that it was likely to lead to universal service on the continental model). Its alternative plan was a National Citizen Army, free from martial law, which would serve both for national defence against a foreign enemy and defence of the workers' interests against the capitalists (a point that was never cleared up was how, in a major war "national defence" could be distinguished from the defence of imperial plunder).

The arguments for a citizen army were clearly summarised by Harry Quelch in the *Socialist Annual* for 1906:–

> Admitting the inevitability of armaments under present circumstances, we have to consider how those can be placed under the most democratic control, be least inimical to peace, be most economical and efficient and least capable of being used by the master class either for foreign aggression or domestic oppression. It is with these objects in view that we Social Democrats advocate the abolition of all standing armies and the establishment of a National Citizen Force; no mercenary soldiery – divorced from civil life, maintained in barracks, a mere military machine, a professional army, a tool and instrument in the hands of the master class – but the whole Nation armed – every citizen a soldier, but every soldier also a citizen; every man in the Nation trained from his youth up to the use of arms, well developed, well educated physically and mentally, and fully equipped and able to play his part in the defence of the national territory against foreign aggression or of popular rights against the domestic tyrant.

The principle of a citizen army was not supported by the other socialist bodies, particularly the ILP whose principal spokesman on the subject – Bruce Glasier, editor of the *Labour Leader* – could not or would not see any important difference between a citizen army and conscription. There were also prominent critics within the SDP, notably Herbert Burrows and J. B. Askew (then London correspondent of *Vorwärts*). The latter argued that, while they held power, the ruling class would decide what was necessary for national safety and that "a democratic army in the hands of a class government must be a fraud".

In the main, however, there was general agreement on the question and when, in 1907, Mr. Haldane submitted to the House of Commons his Territorial Reorganisation scheme, it was regarded as a golden opportunity for bringing to public notice the SDP's alternative plan.

The Executive Committee issued manifestos and leaflets on the subject, leading up to a big demonstration in Trafalgar Square, where a large audience carried with enthusiasm a resolution "To protest against Mr. Haldane's attempt to militarise the nation and to demand the establishment of a National Citizen Force as the only safeguard against Conscription". The speakers were W. H. Humphreys (Chairman), ex-Sergt.-Major Edmondson, Will Thorne MP, J. G. Butler and C. N. L. Shaw of the Clarion Scouts. In addition organised heckling took place at gatherings held for the purpose of boosting the Haldane Scheme.

The driving force in the campaign was ex-Sergt.-Major Edmondson whose expert knowledge of military affairs fully qualified him to speak and write with authority. In the course of two years he addressed over 100 meetings in support of the abolition of the existing military system, besides contributing many informative articles to *Justice* explaining the proposals for a citizen army.

In 1908 Will Thorne presented to the House of Commons a Bill embodying proposals for the establishment of a National Citizen Army. Its main provisions were as follows:–

> Military training to be compulsory for all male subjects of the United Kingdom, subject to certain exceptions.
>
> Training to be for national defence only.
>
> Scheme to be administered by a central board, elected on a district basis by elected nominees from the regiments.
>
> Men to serve 48 days from 18 to 19, 30 days from 19 to 20 and 14 days per annum thereafter until reaching 29th year; trained men of 30-45 to be on reserve.
>
> Privates to be paid 6/- per day, corporals 7/- and higher NCOs 7/6.
>
> Lower officers to be elected by ballot, subject to educational tests; higher officers to be promoted by merit, subject to approval by ballot of the men in the command; facilities to be given lower officers to enter a staff college.
>
> Every member of Citizen Force to be provided with arms and equipment which he shall retain in his own possession.

Members of Citizen Force to retain all civil rights to be dealt with by civil law.

Forces not to be called out to act in any case of civil disturbance.

All members to be entitled, in case of injury, to compensation under the Workmen's Compensation Act.

While, from a distance of nearly 50 years, some of these proposals may appear rather naive (and certainly not all of them – e.g. the election of officers and the short terms of annual service – have been found practicable in the armies of socialist countries) the broad principles behind the Bill were sound and took into account the realities of the class struggle. True, from a realistic point of view, it might be argued (1) that such a scheme could only achieve its object if operated by a workers' government and (2) that it represented too big a jump from the status quo to have any chance of success, failing a radical change in the general relation of class forces; but these objections lose their validity if the proposals are regarded from a propagandist angle, i.e., as a means of bringing home to many who had not realised it before the class basis of the existing military system. Whether or not the Bill was so intended, the fact remains that it supplied the material for much fruitful discussion among the various schools of British socialist thought on a much neglected though vital subject. In particular, it provided the basis on which Edmondson conducted a lengthy controversy with the editor of the *Labour Leader* in the course of which he defended Thorne's proposals with his usual skill.

It need scarcely be added that the Bill did not get very far; but it had a stimulating effect. That, less than 10 years later, its author should have developed into the Colonel of a Pioneers Battalion (old Army style) is one of the ironies of history.

Although no other campaigns that could be regarded as of national importance took place during this period, there were of course, many local struggles around such issues as municipal enterprise, direct employment by local authorities, housing of the workers etc. (of which the Lambeth housing investigation, previously described, is a good example). Also, as was inevitable with propagandist bodies, branches found themselves from time to time involved with the authorities in fights for free speech. Reference is made to a number of such cases in the following extracts from Annual Reports of the Executive Committee:–

> At Plymouth our comrades have been successful in establishing their right to hold meetings equally with other bodies at Stonehouse, in connection with which comrades Tamlin, Parker, Edwards and Rennols, underwent imprisonment. At Nelson Comrades Chapman

and Marklew suffered imprisonment and Chapman–who is Secretary of the Nelson Branch – subsequently appeared before the magistrates and was committed to the Sessions. In this case the police made themselves ridiculous by stating that they would not object to meetings in Cross Street, Nelson, if the Town Council gave permission. The Town Council, when approached, replied that they had no objection to the meetings but that they had no control over the police which is a County Force. Legal assistance had to be engaged, as the police put in a charge of being a common nuisance, which they withdrew when the case came before the Sessions, leaving only the charge of obstruction to be dealt with, for which Comrade Chapman has bound over to keep the peace. Our Nelson comrades will renew the contest when the open-air season begins. Foreseeing the possibility of further attempts being made to treat Socialists differently to other bodies, in regard to street meetings, we made an appeal for volunteers prepared to undergo imprisonment and we are glad to say that the appeal has been well responded to.
(EC Report to 1907 Conference).

Our Sheffield comrades were engaged for many weeks last year in a struggle for freedom of Socialist speech in their parks. The City Council under a bye-law respecting the granting of permission for meetings interpreted their powers to mean the prohibition of meetings. A number of comrades were summonsed and among those who underwent imprisonment were G. H. Fletcher, S. Elsbury and E. E. Hunter.
(EC Report to 1909 Conference).

Last but not least, we must not overlook the hundreds of election campaigns, parliamentary and local, in which the SDF took part, all of which brought to the front both the broad issue of socialism-vs.-capitalism and whatever items in its immediate programme were relevant to the existing situation.

As is well known the SDF (due to its isolation from the broad political Labour movement) was never a great success in the parliamentary field. Its best year in this respect was 1906 when the aggregate vote of its nine candidates (including Will Thorne) amounted to 29,810, an average of 3,726 per candidate (making allowance for the two-membered constituency of Northampton). Will Thorne, the only one elected (with official Labour support) polled 10,210. The figures of the others were: T. Kennedy (N. Aberdeen) 1,934; D. Irving (Accrington), 4,852; E. R. Hartley (E. Bradford) 3,090; H. M. Hyndman (Burnley) 4,932; J. Jones (Camborne) 109; J. Williams and J. Gribble (Northampton), 2,537 and 2,361 respectively; H. Quelch (Southampton) 2,146.

The figures for the two general elections fought in 1910 were still less encouraging. These results, however disappointing from the Parliamentary standpoint, did not, of course, detract from the propaganda value of the contests.

In the municipal sphere, the position was much better; for reports indicate that at no time between 1903 and 1910 did the SDP lack a considerable representation on local bodies (though far smaller than in the case of the ILP). Soon after the organisation had assumed the title of Social Democratic Party, the following municipal programme was adopted:–

The organisation of unemployed labour upon useful work.

The creation and development of Works Departments, so that all municipal work may be done without the intervention of contractors.

Eight hour day, TU rates of wages and a minimum of 30/- per week for all municipal workers.

The erection of healthy dwellings for the workers to be let at rents to cover cost of construction and maintenance alone.

Education to be free and secular with state maintenance of school children.

Most of these demands had, of course, been the subject of agitation for many years past.

To the 1907 Conference it was reported that, during the preceding year, the total poll at local elections was 50,601 with a net gain of 17 seats. At that date the number of SDP members holding positions on councils and boards of various kinds was 100, made up as follows:–

City and Town Councillors	43
Urban District & Parish Councillors	18
Guardians	24
Metropolitan Borough Councillors	2
Parish Councillors (Scotland)	4
Members of School Boards (Scotland)	7
Members of Burial Boards	2

Among the best known of the above were:–

City & Town Councillors: C. A. Glyde and E. R. Hartley (Bradford); D. Irving (Burnley); A. C. Bannington (Coventry); J. Gribble (Northampton); P. W. Llewellyn (Plymouth); A. A. Purcell (Salford); J. Jones & Will Thorne MP (West Ham).

Urban District Councillor: P. H. Gorle (Watford)

Guardians: J. A. Cunnington and Mrs. Ben Tillett (Bristol); D. Irving (Burnley); T. Lewis (Southampton).

Other prominent social democrats who occupied public positions at some time during this period were E. C. Fairchild of Hackney and A. A. Watts of Poplar. In 1909, 6 SDP candidates were returned for the Whitmore Ward of the Borough of Shoreditch.

As far as home affairs are concerned, this concludes our survey of the main achievements of British social democracy between 1901 and 1910. It is submitted that, taken as a whole, they make a substantial contribution to the progress of our working class movement in the comparatively quiet opening decade of this century of social revolution.

Dan Irving (1854-1924)
Source: Lee and Archbold, *Social-Democracy in Britain*

7. The Internationalism of the SDF

As all students of social history are aware, the pre-1914 conception of internationalism, as held by most socialists, was far from universal, limited as it was, both in theory and practice, to the "civilised" inhabitants of Europe, America and what are now known as the Self-Governing Dominions. Thus, when the "Marxists" of the Second International spoke of freedom and self-determination, they had in mind Poles, Slavs, Irish etc. but certainly not the "primitive" peoples of Asia and Africa.

As Stalin wrote in 1921:–

> In the era of the Second International, it was usual to confine the National Question to a narrow circle of questions relating exclusively to the "civilised nations". The Irish, the Czechs, the Poles, the Finns, the Serbs, the Armenians, the Jews and a few other European nationalities – such was the circle of non-sovereign peoples whose fates interested the Second International. The tens and hundreds of millions of the Asiatic and African peoples suffering from national oppression in its crudest and most brutal form did not as a rule enter the field of vision of the "Socialists"... It was tacitly assumed that, although it might be necessary to strive for the emancipation of the European non-sovereign nationalities, it was entirely unbecoming for "decent Socialists" to speak seriously of the emancipation of the Colonies which were "necessary" for the preservation of "civilisation". These apologies for Socialists did not even suspect that the abolition of national oppression in Europe is inconceivable without the emancipation of the Colonial peoples of Asia and Africa from the oppression of Imperialism and that the former is organically bound up with the latter.
>
> (*Marxism and the National and Colonial Questions*)[3]

It would be idle to pretend that the SDF did not share this limited outlook with its opposite numbers on the European continent, not to mention the other British socialist bodies. Indeed, it could scarcely be otherwise, in view of the existing theoretical confusion in regard to the nature of imperialism, in consequence of which colonies appeared as something peculiar to certain capitalist states – Britain in particular – not as an essential feature of capitalism in general; which made impossible any widespread recognition of the exploited millions in the colonies as potential allies in the struggle for world socialism.

In spite of this, there is evidence that the SDP did make some effort to line up international socialism against colonial exploitation. It is contained in the following extract from a report on the Stuttgart Congress of 1907:–

The International Socialist Congress was held at Stuttgart in August. Next to Germany, Great Britain sent the largest delegation numbering 123 and of that number the SDP sent 59... The SDP delegates strove to get the British vote upon all the subjects of the agenda in favour of the revolutionary as against the revisionist policy. The difference in tactics showed itself most markedly on the question of Colonial policy. Edward Bernstein, J.R. MacDonald and others supported the view of the majority of the Colonial Commission, which was briefly to the effect that capitalist colonisation was not wholly to be condemned and that Socialists should take their share in it, if only for the purpose of protecting the rights of the aborigines: whilst the SDP, in company with Ledebour and Kautsky, supported the view of the minority of the Commission that we should be better able to help native races by criticism and opposition than by taking part in their exploitation. This view was accepted by the majority of the Congress. Among the British delegates our attitude was supported by 67 votes to 30 but when it came to the allocation of votes in the Section we were defeated by 14 votes to 6. (EC Report to 1908 Conference)

Evidently something in the nature of a block vote operated in the British Section.

Hyndman, at this time was very emphatic in his denunciations of British rule in India, on which subject he was considered something of an expert, and certainly no fault can be found with the views expressed in the following passage from one of his articles:–

The drain of wealth from India to England yearly without return has mounted up and up and up until now the amount of annual remittances to this country in the shape of pensions, home charges, depot charges, interest, profit, private remittances, freight etc. exceeds £32,000,000... The natives of India are ground down beneath a mean, greedy, galling and vicious despotism, worse even in many respects than that against which the Russians are so splendidly revolting. Not only are they deprived of their subsistence, but all prospect whatever of development in any direction is deliberately taken from them by men of our race who know perfectly well what they are doing and refuse to give up the 'bleeding' of which the late Lord Salisbury spoke. Our permanent policy in India... is 'Divide and Rule'. The British Government never fails to set Mohammedans against Hindus... or to foment the feuds of centuries, which had died down if, by playing off one section of the population against another it can continue to maintain its own hateful and fatal predominance unshaken. (*Socialist Annual*, 1906)

Unfortunately, it has to be admitted that the anti-imperialism of the SDF, apart from its vigorous and uncompromising opposition to the South African War, never went beyond resolutions of protest and expressions of sympathy. Thus, the 1904 Conference condemned the slaughter by British troops of 1,300 badly armed Tibetans; at a big meeting in Queen's Hall Hyndman and Cunningham Grahame denounced the passivity of the Labour MPs regarding the affair at Denshawai (where, in 1907, a number of Egyptian peasants were hanged for defending their holdings against the encroachments of some British officers out hunting); numerous protests were made against British misrule in India, but there is no record of any effective *action* ever having been taken in aid of the victims of British imperialism.

However, it would be quite wrong to infer from its failure to perform a positive role in the colonial sphere that the internationalism of the SDF was a mere matter of lip service. On the contrary, there is ample evidence, covering of the whole period 1901-10, that a very real and practical, if incomplete, solidarity existed between British social democrats and the toiling masses of Europe.

Take, in the first place, the May Day celebrations held simultaneously by organised workers throughout the capitalist world, which were in themselves manifestations of international solidarity. Appeals to sentiment no doubt they were, but sentiment of the right sort has a stimulating effect, which is an important practical consideration. Year after year the contingents of the SDF played their part in the processions to Hyde Park, members taking the day off, often at considerable personal sacrifice. For in those days May Day meant the First of May (it was not until shortly before the First World War that, against the wishes of the social democratic delegates the May Day Committee decided to celebrate "May Day" on the first Sunday in May – thereby destroying much of its significance).

It is worthy of note that among the speakers who address the May Day demonstration in 1903 was Lenin. As is well known, it was about this time that he and Stalin had placed at their disposal a portion of the very limited space of the editorial offices of *Justice* in Clerkenwell Green (now part of Marx House).

Perhaps less familiar to the present generation is the long record of aid and encouragement given by the SDF to the Russian social democrats both during the 1905 revolution and in the tragic years that followed its defeat. Much of this story is told in a series of Executive Committee reports presented to annual conferences between 1905 and 1910:–

One of the most remarkable features of the (international) Congress was the demonstration of international solidarity made at the opening of the Congress by Comrades Plekhanoff and Katayama showing how the principle of internationalism can rise above patriotism, even in its strongest form, such as always comes to the front when two nations are at war.
(EC Report to 1905 Conference).

The S.D.F. has endeavoured to express its sympathy with the revolution in Russia on every possible occasion. The fund to help our Russian comrades started by our comrade Rothstein has realised about £100. The sum may not have materially assisted our comrades in Russia but we regard it as at least an evidence of our solidarity and goodwill. Meetings were held in Trafalgar Square on November 5th and Queen's Hall on November 8th to express sympathy with our Russian comrades in their heroic struggle against bureaucracy and reaction.

In accordance with the decision of the International Bureau, the S.D.F. did its best to hold meetings in sympathy with our Russian comrades on January 22nd in all parts of the country. The elections, however, made it impossible to carry out a series of simultaneous meetings such as had been decided upon by the International Socialist Bureau. In London a crowded meeting was held at the Memorial Hall and co-operation was received from the London Trades Council, the Fabian Society, the I.L.P. (Metropolitan Council) and the Communist Club Meetings were also held in some provincial centres.
(EC Report to 1906 Conference).

The S.D.F. has exercised considerable influence, through our comrade Will Thorne, in preventing the visit of the British Fleet to Kronstadt which would undoubtedly have taken place if the Imperialist Liberal Foreign Secretary, Sir E. Grey, had been able to follow his own bent in this direction. Such gratuitous official courtesy on the part of the Liberal Ministry to one of the worst despotisms that has ever existed shows how much real significance should be attached to Sir H. Campbell-Bannerman's famous declaration 'La Duma est morte; Vive la Duma'.
(EC Report to 1907 Conference)

We are heartily glad to have been of assistance to our Russian comrades who, as delegates to the Russian Social Democratic Party met in Congress last May, after being refused permission to meet in Sweden. The reception given to them at less than a week's notice on May 24th at Holborn Town Hall attracted so large an audience that most of the would-be hearers were compelled to remain outside.

At our suggestion the International Socialist Bureau issued an appeal to the Socialists of Europe to hold demonstrations on July 14th ... in favour of our Russian comrades on whose account the second Duma had been dissolved. In London and the provinces meetings were held on that day to protest against any understanding with the Russian autocracy on the part of the British Foreign Office. At the close of the meeting held in Trafalgar Square a procession was formed to make a protest outside the Foreign Office and a violent and unprovoked attack was made by the police on the crowd. Although tacit consent had been granted, J. E. Williams was forcibly prevented from speaking for the few moments necessary to give point to the protest and to allow of the quiet dispersal of the crowd; Williams and others were roughly handled and 13 arrests were made but only 2 Russians were charged at Bow Street on the following morning; Williams was subsequently summoned for obstruction and fined £2 which he refused to pay.
(EC Report to 1908 Conference)

We opposed the visit of the Czar of Russia most strongly and in doing so we took a course with which not only all Socialists were agreed but which was supported by a large section of all shades of public opinion. Protest meetings were held and resolutions passed against the Czar's visit all over the country. The Labour Party held a demonstration against the visit on July 25th in Trafalgar Square. We had originally fixed upon that date for a demonstration on the Food Supply question... and had obtained the requisite sanction for the holding of the meeting. When, however, it was impossible for the Labour Party to obtain the use of Trafalgar Square on the day first fixed for the demonstration against the Czar's visit, we thought it right to abandon our meeting on the Food Supply and to offer the use of Trafalgar Square to the Labour Party as the demonstration against the visit of the Czar to be effective had necessarily to be held previous to the arrival of Nicholas II at Cowes. Our offer was cordially accepted by the Labour Party and a successful demonstration was held despite the bad weather. Comrades Hyndman, Quelch, and Fairchild represented the S.D.P, at the meeting whilst among other members who spoke were J. F. Green and A. S. Headingly representing the Friends of Russian Freedom. Previous to and during the meeting the sale of "Justice" was stopped by the police and copies of the paper confiscated. Names and addresses of the sellers were taken and threats of summons were made but none were issued. Copies of "Justice" were afterwards seized in two or three parts of London. Comrade Will Thorne put questions in the House of Commons regarding the visit of the Czar and the seizure of "Justice" by the police. No satisfaction could be obtained from the

Liberal Government, notwithstanding that the Liberal Party are supposed to be strict upholders of the Liberty of the Press.
(EC Report to 1910 Conference)

In this connection it is also worthy of note that the holidaymakers at Caister Socialist Camp, mainly ILP or SDP members, celebrated the landing on British soil of His Imperial Highness, Nicholas the Last by pulling down their red flag and flying a black one in its place.[4]

This record of public work in support of the struggles of a brother party is one of which no militant socialist body need be ashamed. However, it is not the whole story. There were other forms of assistance, still more practical, which, for obvious reasons, could not at the time be proclaimed from the housetops. Details concerning them were disclosed many years later by H. W. Lee in the chapter of *Social Democracy in Britain* headed "Gun Running for Russian Revolutionaries".

These activities were not, of course, conducted by the SDF as such but by a body called the Friends of Russia Movement; but it is clear, from Lee's account, that most of its active spirits were social democrats.

It appears that contact was established, through John Leslie, a well-known SDF member from Edinburgh, with a Lettish Social Democrat known as "Alf" who wanted arrangements made for the storing and smuggling of small arms and ammunition to Russian ports. According to Lee's account:–

> Some preliminary work appears to have been carried on by members of the S.D.F. in Glasgow though probably they had little notion at the time of what would be the upshot of their work. After the Russo-Japanese war of 1904 had ended so disastrously for the Muscovite Empire, some new Russian battleships were built on the Clyde. Quantities of revolutionary literature in Russian were quietly but effectively distributed among the sailors sent from Russia to commission the new warships. A good deal of the literature passed through the hands of James Burnett, then Secretary of the Scottish District Council of the S.D.F. Burnett also had a good deal to do with freight notes and invoices, and with giving instructions about when and where the cases were to be taken when it was necessary to arrange their secret transference from the vessels which brought them, and their secret storage till opportunity offered for their safe removal to the ships which would take them to the Russian ports...
>
> "Alf" soon got to work... It was not long before consignments of small arms and munitions began to arrive at Blyth, Sunderland and North Shields. "Alf" in turn visited Methil, Leith, Bo'ness, Grangemouth and the Clyde for the purpose of smuggling the cases and packages on board ships trading between these ports and Russian

ports on the Baltic. This work was going on merrily in the autumn of 1905. (p. 149)

The smuggling went on for over a year. Remarkable skill and ingenuity seems to have been displayed by both parties concerned in outwitting the police and preventing the supplies from falling into the wrong hands. Only once did the smugglers face a serious prosecution. This was when four Scottish comrades – John Leslie, Thomas Edgar, William McKie and W. C. Angus – were charged before the Sheriff Court at Edinburgh with being in possession of explosives for illegal purposes. Here is Lee's description of the trial:–

> The trial came off in due course in the Sheriff Court at Edinburgh before Sheriff Maconochie. Mr. Thomas Shaw was Lord Advocate in the Liberal Government of Sir Henry Campbell-Bannerman. Proceedings were taken under the Act of 1885 passed in connection with the dynamite outrages at that time and the indictment against the defendants was issued from the Scottish Office. The minimum sentence for being in possession of explosives under that Act was 14 years! Feeling they were in for it, the defendants – wisely as it turned out – decided that they would tell the purpose for which the arms and munitions were being handled and defend it. They asserted that there was no intention of using them in this country but that they were simply for shipment to Russia. The 15 boxes found in the raid on the cycle shop at Leith were opened and the cordite taken from the cartridges in some of the boxes.
>
> The Sheriff before whom the case was tried was a strong Tory, not altogether free from political bias, and he did not scruple to criticise the indictment of the Liberal Lord Advocate in anything but a friendly fashion. This was all to the advantage of the defendants. The charge was ultimately reduced to one of having stored explosives in a place not licensed for keeping them and the defendants were fined one guinea for every pound of explosives stored. As the total weight of the cordite discovered was under a pound they were each fined 21/- and costs. (p. 152)

The trial had an interesting sequel, also related in Lee's book.

> Among the things taken from the cycle shop and Angus's home were about a million cartridge clips and 80 Browning pistols. The defendants sought legal advice about the possibility of recovering them from the police. They were told that the police had no legal right to hold them, as the defendants had not been convicted on the charge in the indictment. They tried to get a licensed place in which to store them but, failing to do so, they went to the Central Police

Station, demanded the return of the clips and pistols and got them. They were soon shipped to Russia. (p. 153)

The year (1909) of the nation-wide protests against the Czar's visit was noteworthy for an equally strong demonstration of popular sympathy with the people of Spain. The occasion was the judicial murder, on the orders of the Spanish clerical government, of Francisco Ferrer, a highly respected pioneer of education and free thought. Such a deed was more unusual in those days than during the later period of Fascist terror; hence the reaction to it in progressive circles here was one of shocked horror. In these circumstances, the Secretary of the SDP (the indefatigable H. W. Lee) displayed commendable initiative in booking Trafalgar Square for the following Sunday; so that, within 48 hours of the arrival of the news of the tragedy, Londoners were given an opportunity of voicing their indignation.

The demonstration was a great success. At least 10,000 attended, trade unions with their banners, branches of the SDP and other bodies with improvised flags bearing appropriate slogans. Among the numerous speakers were Victor Fisher (SDP) and R. B. Cunningham-Grahame, freelance socialist and expert on Spanish politics.

At the conclusion of the meeting the demonstrators formed up with the intention of marching to the Spanish Embassy; but they did not all arrive there. A section of the procession was suddenly attacked in Whitehall by the police who, besides other acts of brutality, seized as many banners as they could reach and broke the flag poles across their knees. So provocative, indeed, was their behaviour that normally staid and respectable citizens were heard to indulge in quite uncharacteristic bursts of profanity.

Many meetings were also held in other parts of the country.

Their efforts on behalf of the peoples of Russia and Spain made up the highlights of the Internationalism of British social democrats. In relation to events and developments elsewhere truth compels us to admit that it was a matter of words rather than deeds.

Expressions of sympathy and support were, from time to time, conveyed to strikers in France, Belgium and the United States; and when "Big Bill" Haywood who, along with other members of his union, was the victim of one of the periodical "frame-ups" so characteristic of American capitalism, visited this country he was given an enthusiastic reception by British social democrats.

Fraternal greetings were frequently conveyed by delegates from the SDF to the annual conferences of brother parties on the continent. In the case of Germany, numerous protests were made by both parties against the war plans of their respective ruling classes. Unfortunately, something more than pronouncements of friendship between the peoples was needed to stave off the impending calamity.

The manifestations of internationalism outlined above may not have reached the level of those which followed the first big breach in the chain of imperialism. Yet, bearing in mind the immaturity of the world socialist movement, they contain enough of genuine solidarity to be worthy of the grandchildren of the generation of British workers that rolled General Haynau in the mud.

8. The Birth of the British Socialist Party

As the Amsterdam International Congress held in August 1904 the following resolution was passed:–

> Congress declares that, in order that the working class may be able to exercise its struggle against capitalism, it is essential that in every country there should be but one Socialist Party as there is but one proletariat opposed to the capitalist parties.
>
> For this reason it is the imperative duty of all comrades, Socialist groups and organisation to strive to the fullest extent to realise this Socialist Unity upon the basis of principles laid down by International Congresses in the interests of the international proletariat as against those who are responsible for the fatal consequences arising from the continuance of divisions in their ranks.
>
> The International Socialist Bureau and those national parties where unity exists, therefore, gladly offer their services and co-operation for the attainment of this unity.

As far as the movement in Britain was concerned, it was clear that no combination of forces would meet the requirements of the Amsterdam resolution unless it involved the fusion of the SDF with the ILP. Unfortunately all attempts to bring about an understanding between the two bodies to this end were abortive. This was not difficult to understand in view of the irreconcilable attitude of each towards the most vital practical issue that separated them, viz. relations with the Labour Party. On the one hand, affiliation to the Labour Party was an integral part of ILP policy; on the other, the SDF regarded association with a non-socialist body as a surrender of socialist principles. Since a combination including both SDF and ILP could not be half in and half out of the Labour Party, it followed that no such combination was possible unless one or the other gave way.

No doubt this consideration was in the minds of those members who advocated re-affiliation of the SDF to the Labour Party; but the door to further negotiations was closed when the proposal was decisively defeated at the 1908 Conference. So the various fragments of British socialism continued to drift along separately pursuing more or less contradictory policies.

However, the electoral set-backs suffered by all sections in 1910 demonstrated, as never before, the pressing need for socialist unity. Unfortunately, the atmosphere created by the general disillusionment with the Parliamentary Labour Group, rendered hopeless any revival of the issue of affiliation. Nevertheless, there was a widespread feeling among SDP members that, even if complete unity was not possible at the moment, a determined effort should at least be made to unite as many fragments as possible. It was in this mood that the delegates assembled at the 1911 party conference resolved to call a broader conference "to consider the union of all Socialist bodies and branches into one organisation".

The Unity Conference resulting from this decision was held at Manchester on September 30th and October 1st 1911. During the period of preparation valuable support was rendered by the *Clarion* in whose columns Victor Grayson appealed for recruits to the new organisation. Hundreds of names of potential members were collected – in the case of Brixton alone enough were sent in to double the size of the existing SDP branch.

The success of the conference exceeded all expectations and seemed at the time to mark a turning point in the growth of militant socialism in Britain. An atmosphere of enthusiasm and goodwill prevailed and there was very little of the dissension which so often mars such gatherings. While neither the ILP nor the Fabian Society officially recognised the conference, it nevertheless received the support of more than 50 ILP branches. According to figures given by E. Archbold (author of Part II of *Social-Democracy in Britain*) an aggregate membership of 35,000 was represented by 219 delegates, consisting of 86 from the SDP, 41 from ILP branches, 32 from Clarion Clubs and Groups, 48 from local socialist societies and representation committees and 12 from branches of the new party formed in anticipation. In addition, messages expressing agreement with the objects of the Conference came from 18 SDP branches, 18 ILP branches, 4 Clarion Groups and 3 socialist societies; while letters wishing the conference success were received from Walter Crane and the Socialist Parties of France, Belgium, Romania and Austria.

In deference to the strongly expressed feelings of the delegates, Hyndman, with some reluctance, took the chair and, in opening the proceedings, declared that "he was present not as a Social Democrat, but simply as a common or garden Socialist, wishing to see the union of all Socialist forces in the country". The main resolution, moved by Quelch was as follows:–

> This Conference of Socialist Organisations, believing that the differences of opinion and the adoption of dissimilar tactics which have hitherto characterised the various sections of the British Socialist Movement, have arisen from circumstances peculiar to its initial stages, is convinced that the time is now ripe for the formation of a United Socialist Party, and the delegates pledge their

organisations to co-operate in the unification of their forces on the following basis of common agreement:–

"The Socialist Party is the political expression of the Working Class Movement, acting in the closest possible co-operation with the industrial organisations for the socialisation of the means of production and distribution - that is to say - the transformation of capitalist society into a collectivist or communist society. Alike in its objects, its details and in the means employed, the Socialist Party, though striving for the realisation of immediate social reforms demanded by the working class, is not a reformist but a revolutionary Party, which recognises that social freedom and equality can only be won by fighting the class war through to the finish and thus abolishing forever all class distinctions."

The only amendment to this which was accepted by the conference was one from the Woolwich ILP calling for the deletion of the words "Though striving for the realisation of immediate social reforms demanded by the working class" and the original motion, as amended, was carried amid scenes of wild enthusiasm.

So the British Socialist Party made its appearance on the political stage and the SDP which, under different names, had remained intact as an organisation for 30 years, passed into history.

Before dispersing the conference elected a Provisional Committee made up as follows:– H. M. Hyndman (Chairman), H. W. Lee (Secretary), Leonard Hall, F. Hagger, Victor Grayson, Tom Groom, E. C. Fairchild, D. Irving, Russell Smart, T. Kennedy, Hunter Watts and George Simpson.

The first task of the committee was to draw up a statement of objects and methods for submission to the first conference of the new party. This was the result of their efforts:–

OBJECT – The object of the British Socialist Party is the establishment of the Co-operative Commonwealth – that is to say, the transformation of capitalist competitive society into a Socialist or Communist Society.

IMMEDIATE ACTION – The British Socialist Party supports all measures that tend to protect the life and health of the workers and to strengthen them in their struggle against the capitalist class.

METHODS – The education of the people in the principles of Socialism. The closest possible co-operation with industrial organisations tending towards the socialisation of production and the advocacy of the industrial unity of the workers as essential for effective organisation to that end.

> The establishment of a Socialist Party in Parliament and on local bodies completely independent of all parties which support the capitalist system.

No doubt this falls far short of what, today, would be considered a satisfactory statement of the outlook of a revolutionary workers' party. Among its obvious defects may be mentioned:–

> (1) The terms "Socialist" and "Communist" are used as though they were interchangeable.

> (2) While the "Co-operative Commonwealth" is referred to there is no recognition of the role of the actual consumers' co-operative movement.

> (3) Most serious of all, the workers' political party is not seen as the potential vanguard in *all* phases of the class struggle.

However, these criticisms apply equally to almost all the socialist parties of that day, and in any case, a workers' party must, in the long run, be judged on its achievements rather than its declarations.

Justice was taken over as the weekly and the *Social Democrat* (renamed *British Socialist*) as the monthly organ of the new party.

The first conference of the BSP as such was held at Manchester in May 1912. Its main business was the adoption of a constitution and the provisional one was accepted subject to a few minor amendments. The membership of the party at the date of this Conference was estimated at 40,000, organised in 370 branches.

As well as greatly increased numerical strength, this fusion of forces had the effect of placing at the disposal of militant British socialism a wealth of new talent, literary, oratorical, organisational and social.

First, there was Victor Grayson who still enjoyed great popularity as an orator and was also gaining experience as a journalist. In addition, to name but a few, were the ex-ILPer Leonard Hall and Russell Smart, both eloquent speakers and competent journalists; Tom Groom, organiser of the Clarion cyclists; Fred Hagger, secretary of the Clarion Van organisation and regular MC at the annual reunions at Horticultural Hall; Arthur Rose, an actor whose dramatic skill gave added force to his popular lectures on socialism in Brockwell Park; F. L. Kehrhahn, an able propagandist of German extraction who spent the closing years of the First World War in Brixton gaol; and the Rev. W. B. Graham who lost his job through supporting Grayson and was described by Robert Blatchford as "6 feet of Socialist, 5 inches of parson".

But perhaps the most striking personality among the newcomers was George Moore-Bell, another ex-ILPer from Woolwich who, unlike most of his former associates, was a staunch Marxist. (Even in his ILP days he would follow up statements concerning the grim facts of life under capitalism with the terse comment: "And there are lunatics who tell us that there is no class war.") Possessed of an unusually powerful voice and a delivery that was slow, deliberate and confident, his platform style was terrific, seeming literally to overwhelm all opposition. Rightly or wrongly, he had no time for the more fatuous type of question put to socialist speakers at that time; and when asked "What would you do with the man who won't work?", his reply was short and sharp – "Put his head in a bucket".

Nor was he a respecter of persons. My father who, in 1912, sat on a committee which included both Moore-Bell and Hyndman, used to relate an amusing incident in this connection. A favourite platform trick of Hyndman's was to give a loud "Ba-ah" to indicate his contempt for what he considered the sheep-like qualities of the British working class. On one occasion he rather overdid this performance. At the next meeting of the said committee Moore-Bell took the old man to task, telling him in the frankest terms that it was time these undignified public exhibitions ceased. For several minutes he laid down the law in stentorian tones and for once Hyndman was unable to get a word in edgeways. When at last the tirade came to an end, all he could find to say was "Well, don't break the drum of my ear".

With this galaxy of fresh talent, the veterans of social democracy, a host of new recruits bursting with hope and enthusiasm and a total membership of 40,000 it might well be thought that the BSP at its inception was fully equipped to effect a radical transformation in the relation of forces in British politics. That this did not happen in the years that followed can only be explained by the absence of certain factors without which no political party can achieve its purpose – cohesion, discipline and a firm and united leadership.

9. The Great Strikes

The second decade of the twentieth century may be taken as the starting point of an epoch of wars and revolutions which has already torn something like a third of the world's territory and population from the grip of imperialism. As far as Britain was concerned, this stage did not commence with the declaration of war against Germany. For by the summer of 1914 the country had already experienced four years of the biggest strike wave in its history, which showed no signs of receding. In fact, as even sober commentators like the Webbs could write:–

> British Trade Unionism was in fact in the summer of 1914 working up for an almost revolutionary outburst of industrial disputes. (*History of Trade Unionism*)

Between 1900 and 1910 serious strikes were comparatively rare. So quiet indeed was the industrial front, that there were some among the enthusiasts for political action who ventured to raise the question: "Is the strike played out?" Never did facile optimism receive so rude an awakening...

For the summer of 1910 marked the commencement of four years of ceaseless industrial strife more widespread than any yet experienced in this country. The following facts speak for themselves.

In 1908 recorded industrial disputes occurred at an average rate of just over 30 per month. By 1911 the corresponding figure was 75. The monthly rate for 1912 was higher still, while for the 12 months comprising the second half of 1913 and first half of 1914 it had reached the phenomenal figure of 150.

Attempting to explain this sudden revival of trade union militancy, the capitalist press, as usual, put the cart before the horse, attributing the "unrest" to the evil designs of "agitators" while completely ignoring the obvious fact that agitation cuts no ice unless there is something to agitate about.

Needless to say, the agitation in this case had a very solid foundation, viz., the fact that, during the first ten years of the century, the living standards of the vast majority of workers changed considerably for the worse. True, money wages remained more or less constant; but, due to the increase in the world supply of gold, prices in general rose by roughly 10%. In other words, *real* wages dropped by over 9%. The change was at first so gradual that it was hardly noticed; but towards the end of the 10-year period, the workers definitely felt the pinch and were naturally in the mood to fight back in defence of their living standards.

The question inevitably arose – with what weapons? It is easy to reply – with both industrial and political action which, like the blades of a pair of scissors, are complementary to each other and neither of which can be effective if used alone; but, unfortunately social problems are never solved by formal logic. In order to understand the outlook of the mass of British workers at that time, we must take into consideration the impact on their minds of ten years of Labour parliamentarism – the only kind of "political action" they had then experienced.

As was quite understandable, those ten years of largely ineffective political action had given rise to a widespread feeling that political action of any kind had been tried and found wanting. Whatever the parliamentary tactics of the Labour Group had accomplished, they had certainly failed to prevent a drop of 9% in the workers' real wages, which was far from offset by such meagre social reforms as workmen's compensation, old age pensions, school feeding etc. (in any case the work of the Liberal Party). On the other hand, the one unqualified success of the Labour MPs – the forcing of the Trades Disputes Act on an unwilling government – was closely concerned with the right of trade unions to take effective action on the industrial field. In these circumstances what more natural than that the workers should turn once more to the use of their traditional weapon – the strike?

Such tended to be the reaction to events of the plain man in mine, factory and workshop, more concerned with the daily struggle to live than with social theories. However, there was a quite considerable minority who looked beyond the day-to-day struggle to maintain wage levels and sought a means of ending the wage system altogether, and of these a growing number were encouraged by the apparent failure of political methods to see in industrial action the royal road to the destruction of capitalism. Hence the rapid rise of the somewhat nebulous movement which came to be known as syndicalism and for a time superseded socialism as the main bogey of the suburban middle class. (The term is here used not in any doctrinaire sense but as covering all those trends – whether known as syndicalism, industrial unionism or direct action – which, however much their respective adherents might disagree, had the common factor of placing the main emphasis on industrial as against political action).

Thus, both from the standpoint of immediate necessity and ultimate emancipation, the syndicalist tide was flowing strongly. Small wonder that the concern of Labour politicians over the Osborne Judgement was not shared by the majority of the rank-and-file. As for the convinced anti-parliamentarians, they had good reason to welcome it.

Both before and after the commencement of the strike wave, syndicalist propaganda, in its various forms, emanated from a number of different centres.

In South Wales, considerable influence was wielded by the unofficial Miners' Reform Movement whose pamphlet *The Miners' Next Step* advocated a policy similar to that of the American IWW (including "ca-canny"). According to its preface, it was the work, not of one author but hundreds (TU officials, executive members and workers in the pits).

The SLP in Scotland continued their efforts to spread the ideas of Daniel De Leon.

Industrial unionism had quite a following among the London postal workers, especially the lower-paid sections whose experience of work in a government department was not calculated to incline them favourably towards "state socialism".

The students at the Central Labour College were strongly imbued with the spirit of the "new insurgent unionism". A wealthy patron of the college maintained a syndicalist lecturer – W. F. Hay – on a long propaganda tour of the northern coalfields, besides financing in Glasgow an anarcho-syndicalist weekly – which contained articles by the future secretary of the Miners' Federation, A. J. Cook.

Last, but not least, was the movement that developed around the personality of Tom Mann who returned to this country in 1910 after an absence of nearly 9 years. Although at one time Secretary of the ILP, his experiences of class battles in New Zealand, Australia and South Africa had radically changed his outlook with the result that he came home with an unbounded enthusiasm for industrial solidarity and a corresponding contempt for parliamentary institutions.

He lost no time in throwing himself into the struggle and in due course became President of the Industrial Syndicalist Education League, formed at a conference held at Manchester in 1911. But his efforts were not confined to the mere advocacy of syndicalism in general; he was still more active in the actual leadership of some of the biggest strikes. No need to add that his fearless personality and full blooded appeals for industrial solidarity gained him a large following, not least among the members of political socialist parties.

Having sketched the economic and ideological background to what Allen Hutt described as the "Great Offensive" of 1910-14, we can now examine more concretely the outstanding events of those hectic years.

While scarcely any section of workers was not concerned in one or other of the thousands of strikes and lock-outs recorded, the major conflicts were those involving miners, railwaymen and transport workers.

In the case of the miners, the first serious conflict occurred in the Rhondda Valley during the autumn of 1910, when 10,000 men employed by the Cambrian Combine downed tools over the issue of payment for abnormal places in the pits. The fight was conducted on both sides with great bitterness, which, on the miners' part, was increased by the action of the government in despatching Metropolitan Police and troops to the Valleys, resulting in an ugly clash at Tonypandy. Although the strike was inconclusive, it was not fought in vain since it led the Miners' Federation to take up on a national scale the question of abnormal places in the mines.

Local strikes in the South Wales coalfields continued throughout the next year; but meanwhile the discontent had spread to the whole country. In December a conference of the MFGB decided to take a ballot on strike action for the establishment of a national minimum wage (5/- a shift for men, 2/- for boys). The result (declared in January 1912) showed a majority of 445,300 to 115,271 for strike action and by March no less than 1,000,000 miners had ceased work.

The completeness of the stoppage startled the government into action of unusual promptitude and in less than a month the Miners' Minimum Wage Act was passed. This, however, did not conform to the miners' demands as it failed to lay down a definite national minimum but merely provided machinery for determining district minima. A ballot vote showed a majority of 244,011 to 201,013 in favour of continuing the strike; but a delegate conference held on April 6th decided to call it off on the ground that a two-thirds majority was necessary to justify its continuance.

Among railwayman the "unrest" first showed itself early in 1911 when a number of unofficial strikes took place in the North of England. These were mainly due to dissatisfaction with the Conciliation Boards set up in 1907. Discontent on this issue, combined with the rising cost of living and the non-recognition of the railway unions rapidly became general and led to a demand for action on a national scale. The executives of the four biggest unions issued a joint ultimatum to the companies, giving them the alternative of meeting the men's represent-atives or facing a national stoppage. At once the government intervened with the offer of a phoney Royal Commission, failing which military force would be used to the limit to break any strike.

Undeterred by these threats, some 200,000 railwaymen came out. Though not complete, the response to the strike call was wide enough to threaten to bring industry to a standstill.

The government on their part did not hesitate to carry into effect their threat of military force. According to the Webbs:–

> At the instance of Mr. Winston Churchill, who was then Home Secretary, an overpowering display was made with the troops, which were sent to Manchester and other places, without requisition by the civil authorities, at the mere request of the Companies. In fact a policy of repression had been decided on and bloodshed was near at hand.
>
> (*History of Trade Unionism*, p. 529)

It was indeed! – at Llanelly where troops fired on a demonstration of strikers, killing two and wounding many more.

In spite of this the men stood firm and soon the government adopted a more conciliatory tone, even bringing pressure to bear on the companies to meet the strike leaders. Eventually a settlement was reached on the following terms:–

> Complete reinstatement of all strikers.
>
> Immediate consideration of grievances by the Conciliation Boards.
>
> Prompt investigation by a Special Commission of Inquiry of the dissatisfaction with these Boards and the best way to amend the Conciliation scheme.

When the inquiry was completed, the companies again refused to meet the union leaders but the threat of a further strike compelled them to give way. In the final settlement the conciliation boards were reformed to make their machinery more rapid and their scope more extensive while union officials were allowed to act as secretaries (an indirect form of TU recognition).

At the ports also the situation reached boiling point in the early part of 1911. With rising prices and casualisation, the position of the dockers was little, if any, better than in 1889 and they were demanding that their "tanner" be increased to 8d., with 1/- an hour for overtime. Similar demands were being made by the stevedores, carters, coal-porters, tugmen etc. Strengthened by the recent formation of the Transport Workers' Federation out of the separate unions of dockers and other sections, the combined forces of the waterfront men entered the struggle in the summer of 1911. Strikes of unusual intensity took place in London and Liverpool, marked in each case by provocative displays of the mailed fist on the part of the government. Once again the chief provocateur was Mr. Winston Churchill; but his threat to send 25,000 troops to the London docks to act as strikebreakers only served to strengthen the determination of the strikers. The daily demonstrations on Tower Hill broke all previous records, while the numbers taking part in the accompanying marches through the City reached the amazing figure of 100,000. As in the cases of the miners and the railwaymen, the firm stand of the water-front men had its effect. The government abandoned its intransigent attitude and prevailed on the reluctant bosses of the Port of London Authority to meet the unions. The arbitration award that shortly followed conceded most of the men's demands, including the basic 8d. an hour and the 1/- an hour payment for overtime.

In Liverpool, where Tom Mann was the leading figure, some 70,000 were involved in a strike which included seamen and railwaymen as well as dockers, carters and tramwaymen. Here again substantial gains were recorded but not without serious clashes with police and troops under conditions approaching civil war.

Large bodies of troops were drafted into the city and encamped in the parks, while two gun-boats were anchored in the Mersey with their guns trained on Liverpool. The troops fired on a crowd of demonstrators, alleged to be attempting to rescue prisoners, wounding two; but the charging, without the least provocation, of the monster demonstration on St. George's Plateau must rank as one of the worst cases of police brutality on record.

A vivid description of this frightful affair appeared in the *Transport Worker* and is quoted at length in Tom Mann's Memoirs, but the following passages from an account in the more sober and less biased columns of the *Manchester Guardian* should be enough to convey a rough idea of what happened:–

> Even when the crowd was separated into groups the police contin-ued the onslaught. They used their truncheons mercilessly and some could be seen taking deliberate aim at the backs of the men's heads before giving them blows which, despite the din, could be heard yards away. It was when nearly all the crowds had been dispersed that the worst scene of all occurred... When the police charged up the steps, they had the people congregated there in a trap from which escape could only be effected by dropping from the railings to the flags below. Hundreds realised that this was the only thing to do, but in a few seconds the police had won their way to the railings and men, women, young girls and boys were pushed past them over the edge as rapidly and continually as water down a rock. The officers could be seen using their truncheons like flails. Dozens of heads and arms were broken and many shoulders and arms received blows, the marks of which will remain for many a long day and of those who escaped the blows, many were hurt by the fall. It was a display of violence that horrified those who saw it.

It is satisfactory to be able to add that the violence was not entirely one-sided. For, according to the *Transport Worker*, when they had recovered from the surprise attack, many of the strikers fought back –

with their fists. Naturally the authorities did their best to minimise the effectiveness of any resistance to police violence. Hence the significance of the following incident mentioned by Allen Hutt in his *Short History of British Trade Unionism*:

> So alarmed were the authorities that the local Territorials, who included many trade unionists and who at that time kept their arms at home, were peremptorily ordered to remove the bolts from their rifles and turn them in at headquarters.

Hostilities between London transport workers and the Port of London Authority were renewed in July 1912 following breaches of the 1911 agreement and discrimination against trade unionists. This time, encouraged no doubt by the fact that only 20,000 men at provincial ports followed London's lead, Lord Devonport and his colleagues would not budge an inch. Despite some pressure from the government, they refused to give any undertakings on the points at issue unless and until work was resumed. It was this arrogance on the part of the PLA that prompted Ben Tillett to give utterance to his much advertised prayer on Tower Hill: "God strike Lord Devonport dead".

Though suffering great hardships the strikers fought on with characteristic tenacity, and even when the strike committee recommended a return to work, the dockers voted unanimously to stay out (thus effectively giving the lie to the repeated press allegations that strikes were caused by "agitators"). However, the strike was called off a week later.

The early months of 1912 were noteworthy for the series of prosecutions in connection with the famous "Don't shoot" leaflet. To explain their origin it is necessary to go back to the middle of 1911 when an "Open Letter to British Soldiers" appeared in the *Irish Worker*. The gist of its contents is contained in the opening lines quoted below:–

> Men! Comrades! Brothers!
>
> You are in the Army. So are we. You in the Army of Destruction. We, in the Industrial or Army of Construction.
>
> We work at mine, mill, forge, factory or dock and producing and transporting all the goods, clothing, stuffs etc. which make it possible for people to live.
>
> You are workingmen's sons.
>
> When we go on strike to better our lot, which is the lot also of your fathers, mothers, brothers and sisters, YOU are called upon by your officers to MURDER US.
>
> Don't do it.

This was reprinted in the January 1912 issue of the *Syndicalist*, organ of the Industrial Syndicalist Education League, of which Tom Mann was chairman. The matter would probably have ended there, had not an enthusiastic railwayman reader (P. Crowsley) been so impressed that he had 3,000 copies of the "Open Letter" printed as a leaflet which he proceeded to distribute among the soldiers at Aldershot, He was immediately arrested and sentenced to four months imprisonment. His arrest was closely followed by that of the editor of the *Syndicalist* (Guy Bowman) and the two printers of the paper, Bowman getting a gaol sentence at nine months and each of the others six. Commenting on these sentences at a meeting in Salford, Tom Mann, who, at the time of its publication, was unaware of its existence, read out the "Open Letter" and declared his agreement with "every sentence of it". On his return to London he was arrested on a charge of "inciting to mutiny".

These prosecutions roused a storm of indignation throughout the country. Questions were asked in the Commons by Charles Duncan, James O'Grady, and George Lansbury. Josiah Wedgwood moved an amendment to the Treasury vote in order to voice his opposition. Huge meetings of workers demanded the release of those arrested in connection with the "Don't Shoot" leaflet.

It is unnecessary to consider all the tortuous legal arguments whereby the prosecution sought to justify the charge against Tom Mann. Conducting his own case with great vigour and ability, he combined his defence with a scathing exposure of the government's repressive methods, laying special stress on the events in Liverpool the previous year. In the end he was found "guilty" and sentenced to six months in the Second Division, of which, however, he only served seven weeks; for by that time the protests of the workers had secured his release, together with that of Guy Bowman. During the latter's imprisonment the editorship of the *Syndicalist* had been temporarily taken over by Gaylor Wilshire, a well-known American journalist then resident in this country.

The ferment among the transport workers did not end with the London strike of 1912. A year later the arena of conflict had shifted to Ireland, then part of the British Isles. The centre of hostilities was Dublin where 80,000 members of the Irish Transport Workers' Federation, led by James Larkin and Jim Connolly, took part in what turned out to be one of the fiercest class battles of the century. Police terrorism – no new experience for Irish workers – took the form of a veritable orgy of bludgeoning in the course of which two workers were killed and 400 injured. The courage and resolution of the strikers in the face of this terrorism won the admiration of the working class all over Britain, which took the practical shape of a sympathetic strike of 7,000 railway workers and the despatch, through the Co-operative Movement, of a food ship to Dublin. So intense was the anger aroused by the brutality of the Dublin police that there was much talk of arming the workers, which found an echo even among the leaders of orthodox trade unionism. At the 1913 Trade Union Congress, the President (Robert Smillie) went so far as to declare:–

> If revolution is going to be forced upon my people by such action as has been taken in Dublin and elsewhere, I say it is our duty, legal or illegal, to train our people to defend themselves ... It is the duty of the greater trade union movement when a question of this gravity arises, to discuss seriously the idea of a strike of all the workers.

Though the epic struggles of the transport workers, miners and railway-men were the highlights of the Great Offensive, it must not be forgotten that the four years of strikes and lock-outs brought into action all sorts and conditions of workers, skilled and unskilled – labourers, craftsmen, women and white-collar workers.

One of the earliest expressions of the new militancy was the lock-out of the boilermakers in 1910, following a number of sporadic strikes. Such was the spirit of the rank-and-file that several "settlements" arranged by the union leaders were turned down.

In the following June a strike of seamen for a uniform scale of wages, better working conditions and freedom to join the union of their choice brought the shipowners to their knees, forcing them to concede all demands. A month or so later a three weeks strike of women from 24 Bermondsey factories won wage advances at 18 of them. The strike of the London Society of Compositors, made memorable by the publication of the strike sheet that later developed into the *Daily Herald*, took place the same year.

In 1911 too, the much exploited shop assistants who had been fighting for years to end the pernicious "living-in" system commenced a campaign for a minimum scale of wages. It lasted until well after the first European War but a number of initial successes were gained during the period 1911-13, either by strike action or the threat of it. These included the conclusion of agreements on minimum scales with Teetons (Drapers) Hanley, Boots (Warehouses) Nottingham, Cadbury Bros. and 310 hairdressing establishments in Glasgow.

About the same time the National Union of Co-operative Employees a joined forces with the Women's Co-operative Guilds in a campaign for a national minimum, the union concentrating on the retail stores and the guilds working through their local societies to exert pressure on the CWS.

In 1913 the number of industrial disputes in Great Britain considerably increased, though none were on so colossal a scale as the biggest of the two previous years. They included strikes or lock-outs in the building, metal, engineering, shipbuilding and textile trades. At Dudley girl workers came out for a minimum wage of 23/- per week. Strikes involving 50,000 metal, tube, and nut and bolt workers took place in Birmingham and the Black Country; marches to London by three contingents of these strikers were followed by the granting of wage increases and the establishment of machinery for settling disputes.

During the first seven months of 1914 the strike wave showed no signs of receding. On the contrary, as late as July 17th, referring to the twin crises in Ireland and industry, Lloyd George described the situation as "the gravest with which any government has had to deal for centuries". At the beginning of August there were actually in progress some 100 disputes, including a lock-out of London building workers who had resisted for six months with amazing tenacity and a strike at Woolwich Arsenal for the reinstatement of a dismissed worker. By the end of the month this number had shrunk to 20. The outbreak of the European War had saved the government from the peril of civil war.

On the basis of this brief review of the main events in the great industrial upheaval of 1910-14 it should be possible to form some estimate of its value to the working class movement in Britain.

This is not merely a matter of balancing gains against losses in some thousands of separate disputes. As we have seen, some of them ended in the winning of all or most of the strikers' demands, some in temporary defeat, others in compromises. However, the immediate results are relatively unimportant. Of far greater consequence are the permanent effects of the strike wave as a whole.

The most concrete outcome was an enormous stimulus to the growth of British trade unionism both as regards numbers and organisation. In 1910 the aggregate membership of the unions was about 2½ million. By 1914 it had grown to nearly 4 million. (In the same period the affiliated membership of the TUC rose from 1½ to 2½ million). The transport unions gained nearly half a million members, while the membership of the Workers' Union (which organised general labourers) jumped from 5,000 in 1910 to 91,000 in 1913.

On the organisational side there took place a number of important amalgamations and federations. Thus in 1910 several transport unions set up the Transport Workers' Federation and in 1913 three railway unions combined to form the NUR. In the next year an even more advanced step was taken with the formation of the Triple Alliance (of miners, railwaymen and transport workers).

Less tangible, though equally valuable, were the object lessons, both in strike strategy and the wider aspects of class warfare, provided by the experiences of those four eventful years.

In the course of the struggle numerous weaknesses in the trade union structure were disclosed, thus giving a further stimulus to the movement for consolidation.

The enormous numbers engaged in the bigger strikes developed the workers' class consciousness, giving them a sense of power. This was especially the case on those occasions when the solidarity of the dockers and railwaymen forced the government to climb down.

Experiences at the London docks, Liverpool, Dublin, Llanelli and Tonypandy exposed the ruthlessness of the ruling class; at the same time they served to demonstrate the limitations of "direct action", in face of the vast resources of the capitalist state.

The question now arises: What part did the BSP play in the Great Offensive? To which there is only one answer – a very small one. It is not suggested that the many trade unionists in the party failed to support the strikes in which their unions were involved. Nor is it forgotten that at least one member of the National Executive – Ben Tillett – figured very prominently in the transport strikes so much so, indeed, that, for a time, he supplanted Keir Hardie as the pet aversion of the suburban snob element. The point is that Ben Tillett, the dockers' leader was not identified in the public mind with Ben Tillett of the BSP (as would a Communist trade union leader in a similar situation today).

However unpalatable it may be, we have to face the fact that the BSP as such dragged at the tail of the organised workers and, what is worse, the leadership seemed quite unaware of it. For the sum total of its contribution to the struggle, unaccompanied by a word of self-criticism, is recorded in the following passages from the Executive Reports for 1913 and 1914:

> In accordance with the recommendation of the Organisation Com-
> mittee the branches of the Party in the districts affected by the
> Transport Workers' dispute last summer took an active part in
> feeding the children of the strikers, using their branch premises
> and raising funds for that purpose. In addition branches and
> members of the B.S.P. all over the country held meetings and took
> collections for the central fund established at the headquarters of
> the B.S.P. and much distress was relieved and assistance rendered
> to the strikers in West Ham, Poplar, Erith and other districts
> affected by the dispute.
>
> The Organisation Committee were represented on the Free
> Speech Defence Committee, which was formed to provide legal and

other assistance to those who were proceeded against in connection with the "Don't Shoot" prosecutions and a central fund was opened for that purpose.
(EC Report to 1913 Conference)

The Party took a very active part in organising the first national protests against the brutalities committed by the police in Dublin and the men's leaders in the tramway dispute. Telegrams of protest were despatched by the Secretary to Mr. A. Birrell and a magnificent demonstration was held jointly by the BSP and London Trades Council, with the co-operation of the ILP and Labour Party in Trafalgar Square on Sunday, September 7th, which Comrade H. Partridge attended on behalf of the Dublin Trades Council. The branches of the BSP and the Trades Councils throughout the country were urged to co-operate in simultaneous demonstrations of protest and were passed by many branches of the BSP and forwarded to the Chief Party in Parliament. The Party took an active part in the movement which secured the release of James Larkin and branches and members assisted the various funds opened for the relief of the Dublin strikers. Many hundreds of pounds were thus collected by the BSP in aid of the Dublin Strike Fund.
(EC Report to 1914 Conference).

Meetings, resolutions, collections, feeding of strikers' children, protests against police brutality. All excellent in their way and constituting what would be quite a good effort for an organisation of well-meaning sympathisers; but where was the over-all initiative to be expected from a party professing to wage the class struggle?

The lack of a socialist party with a mass following was a tragedy for the British working class. For had their political consciousness been on a level with their industrial militancy, such militancy could have been turned against the warmongers, shortening, if not preventing, the European War and so saving millions of workers' lives.

10. Factitious Unity

To say that the high hopes entertained by the founders of the BSP failed to materialise, would be an understatement. For, in the period between its formation and the outbreak of war, most of its energies were absorbed in internal conflicts closely resembling those which had shaken the SDF ten years before. The situation was aptly summed up in a remark made by Harry Quelch to a gathering of his old comrades-in-arms: "This fusion has only brought CONfusion".

From the first the varied ingredients, especially at top level, refused to mix. Victor Grayson, of whom great things had been expected, proved a complete disappointment. A strong strain of egotism in his character made him very difficult to work with. Hardly was the Unity Conference over than he quarrelled with his colleagues on the provisional committee over the methods adopted for carrying out party work; and, in association with Tom Groom, went so far as to circularise the branches on the subject. Of the seven meetings held by the provisional committee he attended only two, excusing his absence on the rather unconvincing ground of speaking engagements. Thereafter, beyond addressing a few meetings, he made no further contribution to the progress of British socialism and gradually faded into obscurity. Some time during the war, he was reported to have joined an Australian unit, since when he was never heard of again.

A further source of early friction within the party was the woman suffrage agitation and its "War on the Public". The membership of the SDP had been fairly solid in their opposition both to the limited aims and the later tactics of the militant suffragists; but among the newer elements organised in the BSP were quite a number of ardent supporters of "Votes for Women" (on any terms) who were inclined to regard the militancy of the WSPU as an example to be followed. Leonard Hall was specially conspicuous in this respect.

In some quarters, too, there was a revival of the old opposition to "palliatives". Among those to pursue this line were the Brixton actor, Arthur Rose and, for a time, F. L. Kehrhahn. When his attitude was officially repudiated, Rose assumed an injured air and wrote to one of the socialist organs complaining of persecution at the hands of "Leaders and leaderettes".

Comparatively speaking, however, these were trivial matters which, by themselves, would not have seriously impeded the progress of the party. The same could not be said of the long-drawn-out bitter controversy that raged over the relative merits of industrial and political action. On one side were ranged most of the old social democrats who insisted that the primary function of the party was the political organisation of the working class; on the other an extremely vocal section led by Russell Smart, Leonard Hall and George Simpson who were equally emphatic in proclaiming direct action as the main weapon of class struggle. (The fact that the latter were far from being agreed as to what kind of direct action, only added to the confusion).

In the circumstances, a certain measure of disagreement on this subject was only to be expected, and it was, clearly, desirable that the maximum inner party discussion should take place on so vital an issue. The situation was one that demanded organised and intensive discussion at all levels involving the whole active membership, followed by the concentration of the whole weight of the party behind an agreed policy based on the conclusions reached. Unfortunately what actually happened was that, for a period of years, leading members continued to express contrary views, not only in the party press but on public party platforms (turning into inconclusive debates what should have been appeals for support of a fighting policy). Of these unedifying revelations of inner-party confusion, two examples may be cited.

At a big London BSP rally Tom Mann was invited to speak. In his familiar booming tones he told the supporters of political action "You go and play with your politics; we'll get on with the real work". Later in the evening Harry Quelch in his calmer and more deliberate manner replied: "If political action is played out, then there is no reason for the existence of the BSP."

On another occasion (it may possibly have been the same one) George Moore-Bell, after quoting the Budget figures, with special reference to the vast sums at the disposal of Parliament, went on to remark: "There's economic power for you". He was followed by Leonard Hall who proceeded to state the case for concentrating upon direct action. Such contradictions from the platform could not but create in the minds of the audience hopeless confusion as to what the party actually stood for.

Such confusion was increased by the swashbuckling propaganda of the *Daily Herald* which made its first appearance as a fully-fledged daily paper early in 1912. It was something quite new in British journalism, as different from the present "Odham's Daily" as night from day. Backed by a number of wealthy independent sympathisers with the workers' cause and with George Lansbury actively assisting in its production, it was quite unhampered by the restraints of an official organ and, therefore, free to denounce the capitalists with reckless abandon, to support all strikes and to encourage all opposition tendencies within existing organisations. It even adopted a language of its own, rejecting both conventional journalese and socialist jargon and substituting the popular colloquialisms of the day. Announcements that the "kybosh" had been put on something or that somebody was "getting it in the neck" were a familiar feature. The typical capitalist was constantly referred to as the "Fat Man" and the class struggle as the "Fight against Fat". The issue following a statement by Bodkin, the Public Prosecutor, laying down the law about the South African deportees contained a glaring headline: "Who the devil is Bodkin?"

The main appeal of the *Herald* was made to "rebels" – a somewhat nebulous collection of people, apparently embracing all opponents of capitalism in general, but giving pride of place to those in active opposition to the official policies of the organisations to which they belonged. Thus, special applause was given to the syndicalist rebels against the state and the malcontents within the Labour Party, ILP, BSP and WSPU.

Though the 1912 conference of the BSP formally welcomed its appearance, it was too much to expect that a paper pursuing this semi-anarchist line would find favour with social democrats of the old school, many of whom were inclined to regard it as a liability rather than an asset to the working class. In fact, some of them (including Hyndman, Quelch and Kennedy) went so far as to describe it as a "Jesuit Conspiracy" to spread confusion in the socialist ranks. How much truth there was in this allegation, beyond the frequent contributions to the *Herald*'s columns of the two prominent Catholics Belloc and Chesterton, has never been disclosed; but, whether intentional or not, it is undeniable that the continual indiscriminate attacks upon leaders as such did have the effect of breeding a good deal of unjustified suspicion – a fact that must be weighed in the scale against its positive stimulus to working-class militancy in estimating the role of the early *Herald* in socialist history.

Both Hyndman and Quelch regarded the propaganda of the various groups of direct actionists with an antagonism that was apt at times to override their judgement, blinding them to the positive aspects of the great strike movement. Hyndman, for instance, was not content to criticise syndicalism as unbalanced or one-sided but went out of his way to denounce it as "reactionary". As for Quelch, years of controversy with the DeLeonist school of theorists had embittered him to such an extent that any reference to direct action had the effect of a red rag to a bull. I well remember hearing him at a May Day demonstration denounce "Syndicalism, Direct Action, Industrial Unionism and all that sort of nonsense", proceeding to pour scorn on the "Don't Shoot" line of approach to the following effect:–

> "Don't Shoot!" Who orders the shooting? The officers. And who instructs them? The Ministers. And where do they come from? Parliament. Then why the devil do you put them there?

It sounded most convincing at the time. Unfortunately later experience has demonstrated that the problem is not quite so simple,

To attempt, after a lapse of more than forty world-shaking years, to pass judgement on any of the participants in this controversy, would be both futile and unreasonable; since, in the almost complete absence of experience of proletarian class struggle at the highest level, all were, so to speak, groping their way through unexplored territory. In Western Europe, generations of comparatively peaceful progress had given rise to a widespread belief that capitalism could be brought to an end by "democratic methods". Social democrats might proclaim their readiness to use "every weapon from the bomb to the ballot box" but it is probable that few of them really believed that resort to extra-constitutional means would ever be necessary. The vast reserve forces at the disposal of capitalist governments had yet to be fully revealed (though the process of revelation advanced considerably in Britain during the years 1912-14). This did not, of course, apply to Russia where, it could not be denied, the situation called for some kind of revolutionary action to put an end to the Tsarist autocracy; but it was widely assumed that this would have the effect of bringing that country into line with the "democratic" states.

Hence, in the battle of ideas waged within the BSP, both sides reasoned in accordance with the inevitable limitations of their outlook. The enthusiasts for direct action correctly emphasised the importance of industrial solidarity as a factor in the class struggle. On the other hand, they seriously under-estimated the need for, as Shaw aptly expressed it, "getting to the State end of the gun".

The social democrats, on their part, were right in stressing the necessity for political organisation and the limitations of strike action. Their basic error lay in a tendency to equate political with parliamentary action. True, the kind of parliamentary action they had immediately in mind was in the tradition of Parnell, Bradlaugh and Plimsoll rather than of Snowden and MacDonald. Yet, by implication at least they did envisage an eventual socialist majority which, automatically controlling the organs of the state, would proceed to legislate the new society into existence. In other words, they tacitly assumed that it was possible for the working class to "take hold of the apparatus of the capitalist state and use it for their own ends".

How to crush the inevitable resistance of a ruling class, unwilling to be dispossessed, was a question that was scarcely posed, let alone answered. If the social democrats could not reasonably be blamed for this, neither could the syndicalist elements for putting too many of their eggs in the industrial basket.

However, making every allowance for errors arising from an imperfect knowledge of the nature of the state, it is still conceivable that the BSP, by facing up to the realities of the situation, might have shared in the advances made by the trade unions in consequence of the strike wave. Its failure to do so was largely due to the sectarian outlook of the bulk of its membership, expressed in a contemptuous attitude towards the majority of workers who continued to vote for the same class against which they were prepared to go on strike. Certainly this was inconsistent and illogical and, no doubt, extremely irritating to the more or less politically enlightened minority; yet all that it amounted to was that the class consciousness of the workers in the sphere of industry, where the process of exploitation was unconcealed, had reached a higher level than in the political field where the issues were far more confused (surely an improvement upon passivity on both fronts). Faced with this undeniable, if unpalatable fact, the only course open to a socialist party with a realist outlook, was to throw its full weight behind the strikers, trusting to closer contacts with the masses to raise their political level; but such a course would have involved a break with the deeply-rooted sectarianism which for so long had restricted the influence of social democracy in Britain and continued to do so after the formation of the BSP.

A further contributory factor to the party's failure to rise to the occasion was a strong strain of economism which regarded the industrial struggle as primarily a matter for the trade unions that called for no initiative from the political angle.

It is hoped that these various considerations may help to explain why the BSP actually lost ground in a situation where all the objective conditions seemed favourable to the growth of revolutionary socialism.

Direct action was not the only burning issue on which opinion was sharply divided. An equally bitter conflict raged within the party leadership around the vexed question of national defence.

It is significant that on this issue there was a quite different alignment of forces, the leading figures on either side being former members of the SDP. Long before that body ceased to exist Hyndman had become notorious for his outspoken articles on the "German Menace" and the need for a big Navy and was bitterly denounced in Liberal and Labour circles for "scare-mongering". This line of criticism was, of course, entirely beside the point. In so far as his outbursts served the purpose of drawing public attention to the growing danger of war, they were all to the good – in fact the pressing need was for more, not less, discussion along these lines. From a socialist standpoint the objection to Hyndman's treatment of the subject lay in his obvious concern for the victory of his "own" brand of imperialism, should war eventually break out. His critics inside the SDP argued that the defence of the Empire might safely be left to the imperialists but the business of socialists was to take all possible steps to preserve peace (though lamentably little in this direction was actually done).

After the formation of the BSP Hyndman and his supporters continued to pursue the same line and matters came to a head at the 1913 Conference. Frequent clashes occurred on the Executive Committee elected the previous year which consisted, in addition to Hyndman as Chairman, of the following: Victor Fisher, H, Russell Smart, E. C. Fairchild, Dan Irving, H. Quelch, Leonard Hall, Zelda Kahan, Rev. Conrad Noel and Ben Tillett.

Hyndman's strongest supporter appears to have been Victor Fisher (soon to develop into a rabid jingo), the opposition being led by Zelda Kahan and E. C. Fairchild. Opinion seems to have been fairly evenly divided between the two factions but, owing to the illness of Quelch and the frequent absence of some of the others, voting figures fluctuated. At the December meeting the Executive passed by one vote the following resolution moved by Zelda Kahan:–

> Recognising that the armies and navies of modern Capitalist States are maintained and employed only in the interests of the capitalist class of these States: recognising further that, so far as the workers are concerned, there is nothing to choose between German and British Imperialism and aggression, the Executive of the British Socialist Party dissociates itself from the propaganda for increased naval expenditure.
>
> In conformity with International Socialist principles we declare that a war between Germany and England would be a terrible crime against humanity; that there is no cause of quarrel between the workers of Germany and England; and that no dispute which may arise between the capitalists of the two countries is worth the bones of a single British or German soldier.
>
> Whilst confidently leaving our German comrades to bring pressure to bear upon the German Government to limit its expenditure upon armaments and to cease its dreams of Imperialism, we call upon the British Government to desist from its provocative attitude towards Germany, to declare in favour of the right to capture at sea in time of war, to establish an *entente* with Germany and to decrease its expenditure upon armaments.
>
> We further protest emphatically against the policy of secret diplomacy which leaves the people a helpless prey in the hands of a few unscrupulous financiers and diplomats.

The passing of this resolution was followed by the resignation of Hyndman from the Chairmanship of the Party and Fisher from the Executive Committee. However, when the matter was raised at a subsequent meeting, a compromise was reached by the adoption of the following motion (also by a majority of one) :–

> This meeting of the Executive Committee of the British Socialist Party, in view of the very wide difference a of opinion which prevail amongst the branches and members as to the necessity for maintaining an adequate British Navy, suspends its resolution of December 14th, leaving the Party to decide on this question.

So the resignations were withdrawn.

The following passage from its report indicates that the Executive did make an effort to reach an understanding with foreign socialists regarding common action to preserve peace:–

> After the meeting of the International Bureau an informal meeting took place between H. M. Hyndman and H. Quelch from the BSP and Karl Kautsky, Molkenbuhr and Haase, representing the German Social Democratic Party, to discuss the question of Anglo-German relations and a common policy to be pursued by the Parties in both countries.
>
> The British Socialist Party was represented by J. Hunter Watts and Mrs. D. B. Montefiore at the Special International Congress on War held at Basle in November and Dan Irving attended in place of H. Quelch as a member of the Bureau. The BSP also co-operated with the British National Committee in one of a series of International Demonstrations against War which was held at the London Opera House on November 17th.

It would, however, have been more helpful if the report had contained some information as to the results of the informal discussion on Anglo-German relations.

The subject of armaments was debated at considerable length at the 1913 Conference, held at Blackpool and attended by 106 delegates from 85 branches. An attempt to evade the issue in the interests of "Unity" was made by the Tunbridge Wells Branch which submitted the following motion:–

> That, as the British Socialist Party is a Party of freedom, members are free to hold any opinion they like on subjects apart from socialism and any member expressing his or her views on a subject such as armaments does so as a private individual and in no way pledges the Party to such views.

The mover (F. Sedgwick, party Treasurer) urged that party members should be allowed to have their own opinions and be none the less socialists. They must be united on socialist principles and not split on *non-essential points* (My italics, F.T.).

Opposing the motion Peter Petroff (Kentish Town) said it was not a question of the right to hold a personal opinion but what was the view of the party? If the resolution was passed the party would still be without an opinion on this important question. Where was their solidarity when advocacy of armaments increased the chance of war?

F. J. Farrell (North West Ham) said that the workers had no country and the defence of the country was a question for the capitalists. A result of the invasion of this country might be the establishment of the Socialist Republic.

D. Carmichael (Battersea) considered that Hyndman's advocacy of a big navy had been against the interests of socialism here and on the continent. In supporting the loan of 100 millions for the navy he had undone the good work of thirty years.

J. Owen (South West Manchester) while supporting the resolution, was of opinion that a big navy did not concern the workers of this country who had nothing at stake.

F. L. Kehrhahn (Blaenclydach) disagreed with Hyndman's views on the navy but maintained that, first and foremost, they must have socialist unity. He was prepared to accept a referendum of the party as well as to vote for the resolution.

Zelda Kahan (Haggerston) pointed out that the socialist parties throughout the world regarded the subject of armaments as one closely connected with socialist theories and principles. The working classes had to endure the full horrors of war and were the first to feel the pinch of extra taxation. She recognised fully the good work Hyndman had done for the socialist movement and knew he was no imperialist but his views on armaments made people here and abroad think that he was. In support of this statement she read extracts from the German social-democratic press, showing the feeling regarding Hyndman's advocacy of a bigger navy.

Replying to the discussion, Hyndman repeated his well-known views on armaments, but concluded with a statement that, while those were his strong convictions, he would not raise the question in any way that would prejudicially affect the party.

After this announcement the Tunbridge Wells resolution was withdrawn in favour of the following which was carried with only nine dissentients:–

> That this Conference congratulates our French and German comrades on their vigorous opposition to the increase of armaments in their respective countries and pledges the British Socialist Party, as an integral part of the International Socialist Party bound by the resolutions on war of Stuttgart, 1907 and Basle, 1912, to pursue the same policy in Great Britain, with the object of checking the growth of all forms of militarism.

Zelda Kahan and Hyndman then shook hands.

Unfortunately, neither Zelda Kahan nor Fairchild was elected to the new Executive Committee. This was certainly not due to any lack of support for their line but was probably accounted for by the new territorial basis of election – the successful candidates for the Greater London area (H. Quelch und George Moore-Bell) being unusually popular figures,

For what it was worth, the result of the debate on armaments could be counted as a victory for the opponents of the Hyndman line. On the other hand, the manner in which the problem was approached justifies the conclusion that the party membership as a whole had little or no appreciation of the urgency of the situation. How, otherwise, could serious consideration have been given to a proposal to treat the threat to peace as a "non-essential point" on which member a could be left free to form their own opinions (thus placing it on a level with vegetarianism, Theosophy and the Baconian theory)? And why did none question the wisdom of allowing one holding such reactionary views on so vital an issue to remain in the party leadership?

This conclusion is further supported by the absence of any serious effort to find ways and means of averting the impending catastrophe during the short period that remained. It must seem incredible that, despite the presence of the Secretary of the International, the 1914 Conference, held within a few months of the actual outbreak of hostilities, did not discuss the subject at all.

With a view to preserving a correct historical perspective it has been necessary to stress the failure of the BSP to give effective political leadership on the major problems confronting British workers during the three years preceding August 1914. It would, however, be wrong to assume that its record on this period was completely barren of achievement. On the contrary a vast amount of general socialist propaganda work was carried on and a number of useful campaigns conducted on important, if secondary, issues.

Both before and after its passing, a vigorous movement of protest was led by the BSP against Lloyd George's Insurance Act, which was officially supported by the Labour Party (although Lansbury, Snowden,

Jowett and Will Thorne refused to toe the line. The main grounds of opposition to the Act were (1) its probable effects on the independence of the Trade Unions (2) the growth of bureaucracy involved and (3) the facilities for victimisation afforded by the ticketing, docketing and regimentation of the workers. That these fears, if somewhat exaggerated, were not entirely baseless, subsequent experience has shown.

In the party press as well as at public demonstrations the Act was made the target of vehement attack. At one big meeting George Moore-Bell greatly amused the audience by prefacing his speech with the remarks "I hope you've all got your cards with you".

The BSP also played a leading part in exposing what Hyndman called "the infamous conspiracy which has raised the Plimsoll Load Line", thereby endangering the lives of thousands of British sailors. The publicity given in *Justice* and at public meetings to the hole-and-corner methods of government and shipowners in connection with this scandalous affair was much appreciated by the Seamen and Firemen's Union which wrote congratulating and thanking the party for its work.

Another campaign in which the BSP was well to the fore was that conducted in support of the nine trade union leaders deported from South Africa early in 1914 following a strike which had been brutally suppressed by the government of Generals Botha and Smuts. The "strong-arm" methods of these ex-enemies of British Imperialism had transformed them into heroes in the eyes of the capitalist press which poured abuse on the South African leaders whom it facetiously described as "the dear deported" But the *Daily Herald* on this occasion at least, rendered signal service to the whole labour movement by stoutly defending the rights of the deportees, while denouncing in no uncertain terms Public Prosecutor Bodkin who proposed taking drastic measures against them.

The groups of "rebels" organised in the "Herald Leagues" joined with socialists and trade unionists of all shades to give the exiled leaders a terrific welcome which reached its climax in a monster demonstration at Hyde Park. Of the many improvised slogans carried by the demonstrators, the wittiest was one urging workers to "Come to Hyde Park and give Bodkin the Needle".

With reference to this episode the BSP Executive reported:–

> In conjunction with the London Trades Council and the ILP we organised a well-attended demonstration in the Memorial Hall, London, on January 23rd to protest against the proclamation of martial law in connection with the South African Strike, the arrest and imprisonment of Trade Union and Labour officials without trial and demanding the recall of Lord Gladstone.

We were represented on the London Committee formed by the Joint Board which arranged the demonstration in the London Opera House to welcome the Trade Union and Labour officials, deported from South Africa and co-operated with the London Trades Council, the N.U.R., the Dockers' Union and other bodies in organising the magnificent demonstration in Hyde Park on Sunday, March 1st.

As regards general propaganda, most BSP branches, following in the footsteps of the older social democratic bodies, held, during the summer months, regular weekly meetings at street corners, parks or market places. Taking the country as a whole these must have amounted to hundreds per week. They were supplemented, from time to time, by larger gatherings, organised at national or district level, in public halls or theatres (The EC Report for 1912-13 referred to demonstrations held at the London Opera House and the Pavilion Theatre).

The frequent meetings and demonstrations made possible the sale of a considerable quantity of party literature which appears to have covered an extensive field. It is interesting to note in this connection that the *British Socialist* for June 1912 advertised a list of 13 penny pamphlets published by the Twentieth Century Press Ltd. (the company legally responsible for the party press). These included a verbatim report of a debate between Lansbury and Quelch on the Poor Law Minority Report, *Fact against Fiction* by A. W. Humphrey, *Socialism and Human Nature* by Frank Tanner, *Some Dangers which threaten Trade Unionism* by J. T. Brownlie and *Socialism and Eugenics* by G. Whitehead.

In addition some hundreds of thousands of leaflets bearing such varied titles as "Why Are You Poor?", "Why Do I Vote?", "Strikes" and "The Co-Partnership Fraud" were produced for free distribution.

Unfortunately, these activities, though far from negligible, exercised little effect outside a limited circle of sympathisers, and in any case, could not compensate for the party's failure to establish anything approaching political leadership of the main body of the working class.

E. Archbold, author of Part II of *Social Democracy in Britain* and, as far as I am aware, the only writer to attempt a historical assessment of the BSP, takes the view that the party was reduced to futility as a result of the disruptive tactics of the "Anarchists and Impossiblists" who entered its ranks after the Unity Conference of 1911. Had the party ceased to exist in August 1914 there might have been some basis for this conclusion. Actually, however, it continued not only to exist but to fight until its absorption into the Communist Party in August 1920. Later, it is hoped to show that its record during those six tragic years, far from confirming Archbold's verdict, was such as to redeem its reputation as an international proletarian party and win for it an honourable place in British working-class history.

Addendum in Frank Tanner's MS (originally entitled "note to page 79")[5]

Some advance in this respect was made at the 1913 Conference which passed the following resolutions moved respectively by the Kentish Town and Doncaster Branches:–

> The Trade Unionist and Socialist Movements, being two essential expressions of working-class development, the proper function of the British Socialist Party is to lead the working-class in its economic and political struggle; and, whereas the further successful development of the Trade Union Movement depends on a strong Socialist Party, which can be built up in this country only by converting organised Labour to Socialism, the Conference instructs the Executive Committee to organise the Trade Union members of the B.S.P. for systematic work and Socialist propaganda inside the Trade Unions and call upon such members to strive for the amalgamation and federation of existing sectional Unions in each industry and the establishment of a central executive body representative of all the Unions.
> (Carried 40-22).

> That the policy of the British Socialist Party towards the so-called purely industrial organisations is not one of mere sympathy and support but rather of active participation in, both as individual members and as an organisation, the struggles of the Trade Unions against Capitalism and vigorous support to the growing movement that is surely transforming them from mere reformist wage-raising instruments into revolutionary Socialist Unions, having for their object the emancipation of the wage-earner. To that end the aim of the British Socialist Party should be to command the confidence of the Unions as a kindred and auxiliary body having identical aims and, in order to do this successfully, some means should be devised to make all B.S.P. members acceptable and eligible for trade union membership.
> (Carried 48-22)

It should be noted, however, that in each case the voting was far from unanimous and both resolutions were passed with little or no discussion. In any case the decisions were reached too late in the day to be successfully implemented prior to August 1914.

11. How British Social Democracy Worked

Half a century of experience has demonstrated that essential pre-requisite for the victory of a working-class party are (1) a sound theoretical basis (2) firm and united leadership (3) close contact with the masses and (4) a correct estimation of the strength of the contending political forces. However, these alone are not enough to ensure the defeat of the class enemy. This demands, in addition, a form of party organisation capable of swinging the maximum revolutionary forces into action at the decisive moment.

Since, in the early years of the present century, experience of proletarian revolution was a negligible quantity, it is not surprising to find the majority of European social-democratic bodies sadly lacking in the above-mentioned qualifications for success (the great exception, of course, was the Bolshevik section of the Russian Social Democratic Party which, even before 1914, was engaged in a struggle to build a party of a new type). Despite its uncompromising socialist aims and undoubted militancy on a number of important issues, it cannot be claimed that British social democracy was better equipped, either theoretically or practically, than its continental counterparts to face up to a revolutionary crisis. The sectarianism and theoretical weaknesses of the SDP and BSP have been dealt with already. It remains to examine their organisational structure and methods of working, from the standpoint of the needs of a developing class struggle.

Naturally, the rules and constitutions of these bodies underwent numerous changes during the period 1900-1914; but at no time was their basis anything but definitely social democratic – in the present-day sense of the term – differing in no essential particular from that of the ILP which was frankly reformist and "evolutionary".

While social democratic propagandists, rightly, laid special stress on the fact that the worker was exploited in the process of production, it never seemed to occur to any of them that their units of organisation should, where possible, be based on the place of exploitation – the factory mine, depot etc. By common consent branches were invariably organised on a residential basis.

As for democratic centralism, both the term and the purpose behind it were meaningless to that generation of social democrats. Democratic their organisation certainly was in the formal sense. National officers and leading committees as well as branch officials were elected by the members and decisions were reached by majority vote at annual conferences. On the other hand the kind of centralised leadership British Communists are familiar with to-day would probably have been regarded, despite the traditional Marxist aversion to anarchism, as an intolerable attack on members' freedom. This is understandable enough with a body like the SDF which actually described itself as a "Federation"; but the change of title to "Party" after a members' ballot in 1907 seems to have been a change of name only since there is no evidence that it was followed by any substantial tightening up in the organisation. Nor did the BSP differ materially from its predecessor in this respect.

It is significant that the democratic and libertarian constitutions of the SDP and the mentality associated with it did not prevent its leaders acting from time to time in an extremely autocratic fashion, in consequence of which many good members were lost. What it did, unfortunately, prevent was the exercise of the authority demanded from the leadership of a disciplined fighting party. To put the matter in a nutshell, it was a type of organisation suitable enough for conducting propagandist, agitational or electoral activities, but incapable of meeting the needs of a party seriously engaged in class warfare.

This conclusion is well supported by the available evidence concerning the organisational structure of the SDF, SDP and BSP. The results of a detailed examination of their conference proceedings, rules and constitutions between 1900 and 1914, supplemented by some personal recollections as to their operation in practice, are summarised below under separate headings.

Objects. A statement of the Objects, Programme, Rules and Constitution of the SDF is printed with the Report of its 1903 Conference. Here the final aim is defined as

> The socialisation of the means of Production, Distribution and Exchange to be controlled by a Democratic State in the interest of the entire community and the complete emancipation of Labour from the domination of Capitalism and Landlordism, with the establishment of social and economic equality between the sexes.

This remained unaltered throughout the lifetime of the SDF and SDP. In 1912 the BSP declared its object to be

> The establishment of the Co-operative Commonwealth – that is to say the transformation of Capitalist or Competitive Society into a Socialist or Communist Society.

Comment has already been made on the confusion of ideas here revealed.

Programmes. Like Topsy and the British Constitution, the SDF Programme of "Immediate Demands" was a growth rather than a prepared document, to which additions were made as new issues arose. At the beginning of the century it consisted of nearly 50 items, tabulated without explanation, except for a vague preamble. They commenced with the abolition of the Monarchy and included repudiation of the national debt, adult suffrage, payment of MPs and the nationalisation of numerous industries. Its unwieldy proportions had the effect of exciting the derision, not only of the "impossibilist" groups but also of many loyal supporters. The 1908 conference passed a resolution "to consider the necessity of co-ordinating and re-classifying the items in the S.D.P. Programme" but nothing came of this. It finally ended with the winding-up of the SDP, much to the relief, if the truth were known, of most of the ex-members of that body.

The BSP, at its inception, went to the opposite extreme by dispensing entirely with a detailed programme, for which was substituted a brief declaration to the effect that it would "vigorously advocate and support all measures and activities that, in the opinion of the Party, will strengthen the workers in their fight against capitalist interests".

However, on second thoughts, the 1913 conference decided that "it was necessary to have a Programme of immediate social and political reforms and accordingly instructed the Executive Committee to prepare one for submission to the Branches". Unfortunately, the EC had to confess to the 1914 conference that it had not yet succeeded in getting down to the job and therefore for the time being, the matter was left as war broke out three months later.

Whatever its weaknesses, the present generation of militant British socialists can at least claim to have learn something of the art of relating immediate problems to ultimate aims. This is evident from the contrast between both the miscellaneous hotch-potch of unrelated demands which formed the programme of the SDF and the vague generalities of the BSP Constitution and such a document as the *British Road to Socialism* with its clear picture of the successive stages of the developing struggle for workers' power through a Peoples' Government. But here again we must remind ourselves that our grandfathers and grandmothers had no experience of successful workers' revolutions to guide them.

Membership of the social democratic organisations was open to all adults who accepted their aims and general policies. New members were enrolled at branch meetings after completing application forms.

The rules had more to say about what a member was *not* permitted to do than what he or she must do. Those of the SDF laid down (1) that no member could stand as an election candidate, either Parliamentary or Municipal, except as an avowed social democrat and subject to certain conditions as to programme and control and (2) that a member holding office in a trade union or trades council must not give verbal or written support to a non-socialist candidate without making it clear that he did so in his official capacity. (The rules of the BSP adopted in 1913, contained similar prohibitions but in a modified form.)

On the other hand, nothing positive was demanded from a member, beyond the regular payment of dues.

Reference has already been made to the continual passing to and fro of members of the SDP and ILP during the early years of the century. This was not entirely the result of political conversion. For not all members were equally concerned about points of doctrine. Many of the rank and file of both bodies made little distinction between them and were, therefore, ready to transfer their allegiance from one to the other for reasons quite unpolitical (e.g. personal dislikes or removal to an area where only one branch existed). In the period of rising popularity of the Labour Party, this ebb and flow movement operated mainly to the disadvantage of the social democrats; but there was a drift in the opposite direction round about the time of the Unity Conference.

As a rule there was little ceremony or sentiment in connection with the enrolment of new members. A notable exception, however, was the "Initiation Address" which used regularly to be read out whenever a recruit was made to the Lambeth S.D.P. As, in all probability, all trace of this unique document – originally drafted by Olaf Bloch – has long passed into oblivion, it is worth quoting some of its most striking passages. To the best of my recollection, after hearing them read for my benefit on a far-off evening in April 1908, these were as follows:–

> We welcome you to the ranks of the Social Democratic Party... It is not a local event, nor even a National event. It is an international event of importance... The Social Democratic Party is a poor Party because it is a genuine working-class Party. Therefore, we hope that you will pay your subscriptions regularly... And we rejoice that a worthy cause has added yet another worthy adherent to its fighting ranks.

More than one promising recruit was heard to comment on the inspiring effect of this address.

Branches. The unit of organisation in the SDF and SDP was the residential branch, for which the minimum membership required was 6. Needless to say, not many were as small as this. In some cases their numbers exceeded 100. The fact that, included among the "branches" were a number of semi-independent local socialist societies such as the Bristol Socialist Society illustrates the loose character of the organisation.

Branches paid dues to the National Executive and, where such existed, to their district committees and were expected, though not obliged, to follow the general leads given from the centre. Otherwise, they were left very much to their own devices, apart from certain restrictions regarding the running of Parliamentary or Municipal candidates.

Activities of branches varied greatly from place to place, according to local circumstances and the initiative of their members. Generally speaking, they included one or more weekly open-air meetings in the summer months, Sunday evening lectures in the winter and, for money-making purposes, regular or occasional social events. The most active branches were often engaged in local campaigns on definite issues (e.g. unemployment, housing, school feeding) either independently or in association with other local bodies.

In many cases branches were affiliated to the trades councils in their areas. The same applies to local LRCs, though, probably, to a lesser degree, as some branches held the view that it was not logical to affiliate locally while refusing to do so nationally.

Branches were free to elect as many officers and committees as they liked, but there was nothing corresponding to the present Communist Branch Committee with its collective responsibility for leading the activities in the area. In practice, it was usual to elect a branch chairman, secretary, treasurer (or financial secretary) minute secretary and literature secretary, each of whom was left to carry out his own job.

Branch meetings were usually held weekly, the typical agenda consisting of the following items:–

> Minutes
> New Members
> Correspondence
> Reports
> Any Other Business

Discussion on the progress of local campaigns might form a separate item but was often covered by the appropriate report.

Some branches made a practice of following up their business with general discussions on set topics but these seldom had any special local significance and were certainly not regarded as a preliminary to action. For instance, among the subjects discussed at branch meetings of the Brixton BSP were "Determinism", "Socialism and Art" and "The Problem of the South African Native".

The frequency of branch meetings and the red-tape involved in their conduct had the effect of making many experts in procedure, especially among branch chairmen who often tended to be more concerned with getting through the business and conforming to standing orders than with reaching sound political decisions.

Some light on branch life in the SDF of 50 years ago is thrown by a discussion on "The Retention of Members by Branches" which took place at the conference. It was opened by W. Gee, whose remarks strike a very familiar note. He declared:–

> The question most deserving of consideration is not so much how to get new members as to retain those we already have. It is to me an amazing circumstance that the present number of members constitutes a microscopic proportion of the number that have passed through the branches. The conduct of the business of the branches is one of the first considerations. There is such a thing as S.D.F. time for starting business – namely starting late – and nothing is more injurious. Another important thing is that we should try to educate our members and when they come in we should fraternise with them. We should never lose touch with our members but, if necessary, go to them if they do not come to us... Even if we had only one quarter of those who had been members and who were worth having, we should be a far greater power in the political life of the nation.

A piece of self-criticism only too rare in those days!

The rules governing BSP branches were little different from those of the SDF, except that the minimum membership was raised to 10.

National Conferences. In the SDF Rules it was stated:

> National Conferences shall be held annually to decide policy for the ensuing year, make rules, deal with alterations every third year, carry out the Objects and Programme of the Federation, decide all appeals against decisions of the Executive Council and elect the E.C. and paid officials, all of whom shall be nominated by Branches.

The corresponding rules of the BSP were to much the same effect, except that the Executive was given power to appoint national officials.

In the event of important issues arising between conferences, the rules of both bodies provided for a referendum to members, on the initiative either of the EC or a stipulated number of branches.

The basis of representation in each case was one delegate for every 50 members or part thereof. It was usual for conferences to elect their own chairmen.

In practice, these conferences more closely resembled a present-day Labour Party Conference, Trade Union or Co-operative Congress than a Congress of the Communist Party. The main part of the agenda consisted of discussion of the EC's report for the previous year, together with a miscellaneous string of resolutions on the most varied subjects, internal and external, ranging from branch dues to the international situation. Needless to say, it frequently happened that, while comparatively trivial questions received far more than their fair share of attention, really important ones were either very briefly disposed of or not reached at all. Despite this, much conference time was often occupied in somewhat academic discussion of current social problems, leading to no definite action.

Conference debates were not, as a rule, preceded by any *organised* discussions by members either in the branches or the party press, although this did happen in the case of the proposals for socialist unity prior to the 1914 BSP Conference.

Executive elections were conducted on the most formal and casual lines, no lead being given either as to the kind of executive required or the qualifications needed for leadership of a working-class political organisation. Anything in the nature of a Panels Commission would certainly have been regarded as a gross interference with delegates' freedom of choice. This *laissez-faire* attitude towards the selection of leaders, in spite of its surface appearance of scrupulous fairness, actually worked in favour of candidates well-known as speakers or writers, to the detriment of those possessing the less spectacular but equally important qualities necessary for leadership (there was, for instance, no means of ascertaining a candidate's standing in the broader working-class movement). Neither did it ensure the election of an executive whose composition reflected the views of the general membership. A glaring instance of failure to do so was provided at the 1913 Conference of the BSP which, while declaring emphatically against increased armaments, elected an EC of whom the majority proved to be supporters of the war against Germany.

Leadership. The leading body in the SDF and SDP was the Executive Council, consisting of 12 members of whom 6 must be members of different provincial branches (a rule doubling these figures, adopted in 1903, had to be dropped as impracticable). In practice, the London section met much more often than the EC as a whole.

The rules of the BSP limited the number of its executive to 9, "all of whom shall be nominated and elected by grouped areas of Branches". They also provided that "the EC shall not have power to pass any resolutions dealing with the policy of the Party, except it is referred to them by the last Annual Conference".

Subject to these limitations, the various executive bodies carried out party policy. The Secretary never was, nor was expected to be an outstanding leader of the type of Maurice Thorez or Harry Pollitt. His job was to carry into effect the decisions of the executive.

A scrutiny of the Annual Reports issued by the executives of the SDF, SDP and BSP between the beginning of the century and 1914 reveals in striking fashion the conception of socialist leadership which was prevalent at this stage in the development of the movement. Nowhere is it possible to detect the slightest note of self-criticism. On the contrary, one gathers the impression of a determined effort to present the previous year's work in the brightest possible colours, which is amply borne out by the recurrence year after year of such phrases as "The campaign was a great success", "We have every reason to be gratified at the success of our year's work". It is campaigns on unemployment, school feeding and in support of workers' struggles abroad; but in relation to their basic tasks the approach of the leadership was the reverse of dialectic. Never was the problem posed in terms such as these:–

> Have we increased our influence over the workers of Britain? If not why not? What must be done to overcome our weaknesses? And by what means?

Instead, members were presented with a recital of things done, some deserving of praise, others of little significance (including the number of phone calls made and received at the Head Office during the year) expressed in complacent terms and with little or no consciousness of falling short of what might be expected from a body with aspirations to be the revolutionary vanguard of the working-class.

To what extent this avoidance of self-criticism was due to an unjustified fear of exposing weakness in face of the class enemy, it is impossible to say. What is indisputable is that it served to cover up and perpetuate errors rather than to correct them.

District Organisation. Neither the rules of the SDF nor those of the BSP made provision for the formation of any administrative bodies between their national Executives and branches. Nevertheless, sheer necessity rendered it essential that district councils or committees of some sort should be set up in thickly populated areas with comparatively high memberships. So largely in response to local demand a number of such bodies were formed in various parts of the country, though in a haphazard and irregular fashion.

That active interest was taken by the SDP Executive in the efficient organisation of the London branches is evident from the following announcement in its 1908-09 report:–

> The formation of the London Committee last year and the appointment of E. C. Fairchild as Organiser have been more than justified

by the results obtained. Since last July the membership of the Party in London and its suburbs has increased 75%.

The same cannot be said of provincial areas, though by reason of their greater remoteness from the centre, they stood in greater need of attention. This explains a widespread demand, during the concluding years of the existence of the SDP for a scheme of decentralisation, not as a matter of principle but on practical organisational grounds.

The unplanned character and uneven development of party organisation in the districts continued after the formation of the BSP. Even as late as 1913, conference resolved "that the United Kingdom be divided into Divisional Areas with Councils and that the E.C. endeavour to subsidise paid residential secretaries as soon as funds permit".

From the little documentary evidence available one gathers that organisational bodies were formed from time to time in a number of provincial areas (e.g. Scotland, Lancashire, Yorkshire) but detailed information regarding their actual working is extremely scanty.

Concerning London, it is possible to speak with greater knowledge, in view of my own personal experience as an active member of the movement there from 1908 to 1914.

Under Fairchild's able leadership, the London District Committee did much to activate branches on such pressing immediate issues as unemployment and housing. Their efforts in this direction sometimes met with resistance; for not a few members were inclined to regard district organisers and committees as their natural enemies (I once heard an otherwise excellent comrade remark "I don't want anybody to organise me") and branches where this spirit prevailed did not take kindly to what they considered "outside interference". It is only fair to say that the position in this respect was not helped by a tendency on the part of some of the committee to regard branch members either as difficult recruits or wayward children.

The London Committee, whose organisation was carried into the BSP, more or less intact, also rendered a great service to the London movement by regularly supplying speakers for both the open-air and indoor meetings arranged by the branches throughout the area. There were, naturally, occasional failures to fulfil engagements, due to slackness or misunderstanding but on the whole the arrangement worked well. Among the London panel of speakers during the six years mentioned were, in addition to Fairchild himself, Val McEntee, Humphreys of Battersea, Lockwood of Camberwell, R. C. Morrison, E. Archbold, Peter Petroff, Joe Fineberg, Zelda Kahan and Margaretta Hicks.

Finance. In 1903 the minimum contribution of an SDF member to his branch was fixed at 2d. per week. This amount could be remitted or reduced in cases of sickness or unemployment.

Until 1907 branches were required to pay 3d. per member per month to the central office. Then a ballot of members decided in favour of reducing the rate to 1/- per member per annum, as it was found that a number of branches made a practice of deliberately under-estimating their membership to avoid full payment. The result of the change was that in the first few months of 1908, 3 times as many membership cards were issued as in the previous year.

In the BSP it was left to branches to fix their own members' contributions but each member was required to pay 1/- per annum to a Central Parliamentary Fund.

Branches of both bodies supplemented their incomes from the proceeds of socials, literature profits and collections at meetings.

Numerous contributions were made by well-to-do sympathisers to the central funds which were also augmented, from time to time, by substantial payments out of the profits of the Twentieth Century Press.

There was nothing corresponding to branch quotas or members' guarantees, neither was money-raising regarded as primarily a political problem.

However, one distinctive feature of social democratic finance which deserves favourable comment, was the existence of a number of flourishing trading concerns, run on co-operative lines, which were set up for the express purpose of swelling party funds. (This was all the more remarkable in view of the general indifference of social democrats to the activities of the official consumers' co-operative movement).

Of these the most successful were the Pioneer Boot Works, closely associated with the name of James Gribble of Northampton, which for some years contributed an average of £200 to the SDP funds, and Red Flag Toffee, run by the West Leeds Branch of the SDP which, in the space of two years, enabled branches to earn £450, as well as contributing £40 to the Twentieth Century Press.

Both these concerns were taken over by the BSP, together with the other assets and liabilities of the former party, and continued to give sound financial support to the movement.

Shortly after the formation of the BSP two further trading bodies were set up on a co-operative basis, viz. (1) Co-operative Supplies Ltd., formed on the initiative of E. C. Fairchild who became its manager and (2) Advance Trading Stores, under the management of F. L. Kehrhahn.

Press. As already explained, the body directly responsible for the publication of the social democratic press and other literature was the

Twentieth Century Press Ltd. Actually *Justice* was run at a loss but this was more than offset by the profits on the other publications and the firm's commercial work. The other publications included a constant stream of pamphlets, reports of debates, translations of such of the Marxist classics as were then available (in particular *Communist Manifesto, Value, Price and Profit* and *Wage Labour and Capital*).

Like most weekly organs of that period, *Justice* was of the magazine type, much of its contents being devoted to critical comments on current affairs. A very popular feature was "Topical Tattle" actually written by Harry Quelch, dealing with all sorts of controversial issues, many of them raised by readers. There was a lively correspondence column, in which members freely ventilated various grievances concerning the internal working of the organisation. The only part of the paper containing anything that could be called "news" was the International page dealing with the progress of the movement abroad. Beyond this, the only concrete reports were embodied in "London Notes" and a column, consisting of very brief items of branch activities, a typical sample of which might be worded thus:–

> We held a very good meeting outside the Red Lion last Sunday evening, Mr. Jones of the Tariff Reform League being much in evidence as usual. Two new members joined this week.

The branch members responsible for supplying these snippets of information were the nearest approach to local correspondents then existing.

The monthly organ *The Social Democrat* (later *British Socialist*) reviewed the events of the month and contained many well-informed articles on foreign affairs. Otherwise, its contents were mainly devoted to theoretical discussion.

Education. The records of both the SDF and the BSP indicate that no systematic educational, as distinct from propaganda, work was carried out by either body. True enough, in the course of the first 14 years of the century numerous isolated efforts were made to raise the social consciousness of the membership. Over a term of years interesting and informative Sunday evening lectures were arranged by the centre at Chandos Hall. Many similar addresses were given under branch and district auspices. In a number of cases branches organised local libraries, economic courses, speakers' classes etc. or provided facilities for their more studious members to read Marxist literature for themselves. Above all, we must not forget John McLean's historic economic classes which, however, appear to have been conducted for the benefit of workers in general rather that of selected students and, at the height of his fame, assumed the character of mass demonstrations.

The point is that these activities were sporadic and uncoordinated, never forming part of an overall plan to raise the political level of the membership as a whole.

Various aspects of the problem of members' education were raised, from time to time, at annual conferences but in too piecemeal a fashion to lead to any comprehensive results.

The 1907 Conference of the SDF carried by 72-8 a resolution moved by Albert Inkpin instructing the EC to organise educational lectures throughout London and the provinces dealing with the general principles of socialism.

In 1909, it was agreed that steps be taken to form a circulating library on the lines of the Fabian Society's Book Box Scheme. The 1910 Conference called on all branches to withdraw from the Workers' Educational Association.

At the 1913 Conference of the BSP a proposal from St. Helens to endow two scholarships at the Central Labour College for the benefit of party members was defeated by the chairman's casting vote.

There is no evidence that any of the above-mentioned decisions were carried into effect. Even so, they dealt with only minor aspects of the problem of members' education. The pressing need for a comprehensive scheme for the training of party cadres would seem to have been completely overlooked by the pre-1914 generation of British social democrats.

Women's Work. The small minority of women members of the SDF and BSP gave a good account of themselves, though their activities were not always of the highest order and there was too great a tendency to divide the work of men and women into water-tight compartments.

The special activities of the women members in 1907-08 are outlined in the following passage from the Report of the EC to the SDP Conference for that year:–

> The third annual report of our Women's Committee shows that they have had a good year's work. The Socialist Women's Circles are in a flourishing condition and there are now 13 Circles in existence. They are: Northampton, Wellingborough, South West Manchester, Exeter and Stonehouse in the Provinces and Scotland and Bow and Bromley, Willesden, Central, Deptford, Fulham, Hammersmith, Islington and Southwark in London. The Committee have issued two leaflets and the pamphlet "Some Words to Socialist Women". The pamphlet is being translated into Dutch for the women comrades of Amsterdam. The Committee is represented on the

> Socialist Women's Bureau, A section of the Women's Committee have continued their labours in providing the refreshments served at Chandos Hall.

The concluding sentence, which is something of an anti-climax, illustrates a regrettable tendency then prevalent to regard such jobs as serving refreshments and presiding at bazaar stalls as specially suitable for women. This attitude of mind led at times to strong protests from the more enlightened members (men as well as women).

The organising of the circles referred to above, which apparently embraced sympathisers as well as members, seems to have been the main special activity on which women social democrats concentrated. In 1909 their number had grown to 23 – 12 in London, 8 in the Provinces and 3 in Scotland.

In the BSP period the number of circles diminished slightly, 16 being reported as in active working order at the time of the 1913 Conference. On the other hand women's activities appear to have extended in other directions, for the EC reported as follows:–

> As a means of interesting and organising women, the Women's Council have established co-operative clubs which are steadily growing; and a series of exchange essays upon subjects of particular interest to women such as "Endowment of Motherhood", "Food", "Wages and Prices" etc. are in circulation. A Conference held in November for the exchange of views among women was a great success.

There is no reason to believe that social democratic women established any close contacts with other bodies of working women, although the Women's Co-operative Guilds became quite active during this period.

Sunday Schools. An outstanding feature of British socialism in the early years of the century was the Socialist Sunday School, run by the local SDP or ILP (sometimes by both jointly).

Most of the children attending these schools came from socialist families but all who cared to go were made welcome. On Sunday afternoons, they listened to talks on broad humanitarian themes, asked questions, sang socialist hymns, and were instructed in the Ten Socialist Commandments – consisting of purely ethical precepts completely free from dogma or mysticism, which extolled the social virtues and specially condemned national and racial hatred. Annual tea-fights and excursions to the country or seaside made up the lighter side of the programme.

One of the first Sunday Schools was formed by Mary Gray, an active SDF member, at Sydney Hall, Battersea as far back as 1895. By the turn of the century, they had become quite numerous and quickly spread to all parts of the country. Quite a successful one was conducted by Edith Lanchester at the premises of the Lambeth SDF, near Kennington Oval. Later, Edith helped to form another at Brixton. This was supposed to be a joint effort in association with the local ILP but in actual fact, practically all the work was done by SDP members, the most strenuous worker being Eleanor Goodrich, a professional teacher who, many years afterwards, became Mayor of Wandsworth, An occasional visitor to this school was Herbert Morrison, then Chairman of the Brixton ILP.

Other successful Sunday Schools referred to in conference reports were those at Rochdale and West Ham.

While no figures are available as to how many schools were respectively organised by the different socialist bodies, there is no doubt concerning the substantial contribution rendered by both SDP and BSP branches to the success of the Sunday School movement. Even so, judging by the frequent demands at annual conferences that the subject be given greater attention, the enthusiasts for the instruction of children in the principles of socialism were far from satisfied. On at least three occasions between 1905 and 1914 conferences called upon branches to establish Sunday Schools where they did not already exist.

Youth. The social democratic organisations were singularly unsuccessful in attracting the socialist youth. Reports do, indeed, contain occasional vague references to the existence of a Young Socialist League; but, whatever its activities and achievements may have been, they have long since faded into obscurity and certainly made no lasting impression on the pre-1914 generation of adolescents.

The weakness of the movement in this respect was discussed from time to time but no effective steps were taken to overcome it. This is evident from the fact that, as late in the day as 1913, the annual conference of the BSP found it necessary to pass the following resolution:–

> This Conference is of opinion that an organisation is necessary for educating and organising young men and women of the ages of 14 to 21, thus fitting them to take their places in the Adult Socialist Movement; and calls upon all branches of the British Socialist Movement to appoint some responsible members to work in conjunction with existing local Socialist Movements in forming Branches of the Young Socialist League; and instructs the Organisation Committee immediately to draw up a scheme of organisation to be sent to all Branches for their guidance.

As was the case with various other excellent schemes, the outbreak of war the following year prevented these proposals from being carried into effect.

From the above survey of the organisation structure and working methods of British social democracy, it should be clear that, like curates' eggs of inferior quality, they were good only in a few parts. Many years of trial and error were to pass before militant socialism in Britain developed a form party structure capable of fulfilling its historic role.

Harry Quelch (1858–1913)
Source: Lee and Archbold, *Social-Democracy in Britain*

12. Re-affiliation at Last

It was not surprising that the enthusiasm with which the formation of the BSP was greeted by its supporters in Britain, was by no means shared by the members of the International Socialist Bureau. For, to them, the problem of the plurality of British parties still remained and it was of little consequence if one of them expanded slightly relative to the others. As *Vorwärts*, official organ of German Social Democracy, expressed it:–

> What is done by the divided, independent, local organisations who are by no means numerous or strong in membership is of quite minor importance and all permutations, combinations and varia-tions with these varying elements, whether it be by the S.D.P. or the I.L.P. do not yet make up a United Socialist Party.

Objectively, the major problem was still how to reconcile the conflicting standpoints of British social democrats and the ILP and Fabians in relation to the Labour Party.

At first the members of the new party were either too elated with their apparent success or too preoccupied with the problems presented by the industrial upheavals on the home front to pay much attention to continental opinion. However, the experiences of 1912 had the effect of considerably damping down the earlier enthusiasm which give place to a widespread feeling that the results of the Unity Conference had not come up to expectations. It was in these circumstances that the International Bureau resolved to make a further attempt to establish real socialist unity in Britain which took the form of a somewhat peremptory call to the BSP Executive to hold informal talks on the subject with representatives of the other socialist bodies.

The talks in question took place at the offices of the Fabian Society on July 18th, 1913. Dan Irving, Victor Fisher and J. Hunter Watts represented the BSP, Keir Hardie, W. C. Anderson and J. Bruce Glasier the ILP, and Beatrice Webb, E. R. Pearse the Fabian Society, while E. Vandervelde and Camille Huysmans attended on behalf of the Bureau.

The outcome of the discussions was the issue of a statement embodying agreement on (1) the establishment of a Joint Socialist Council and (2) Affiliation to the Labour Party; but more definite action was postponed until such time as the members of the respective organisations had been given an opportunity of expressing their views. It was left to the Bureau to arrange a further joint conference towards the end of the year.

For the next few months the question of Labour Party affiliation was the subject of continual and often heated discussion, both in the BSP branches and in the columns of *Justice*. Among the first to submit his views was Harry Quelch himself who repeated the objections to the Labour alliance which he had voiced for over 10 years. This was the last public statement to issue from his powerful pen as he was already far advanced in his last illness. He died the following September, deeply mourned by all sections of the socialist and trade unionist movement, as the procession of 10,000 which followed his body to the grave eloquently testified.

The discussions on affiliation were carried on with unabated vigour until December when a further conference was called by the International Bureau. The recommendations of the previous joint meeting were supported by most members of the executive as well as by those who, like Hyndman, Headingley, Gorle, Fisher and Hunter Watts, were in the closest touch with continental social democrats. On the other hand, as was to be expected, there was a hard core of opposition, mainly at branch level, including some of the ablest party speakers (e.g. W. Gee, Pearse, Petroff, Walker of Deptford, Tovey of Hampstead and Gil Roberts of Openshaw) which all the wiles of officialdom failed to overcome.

Though there was no question as to the genuineness of this opposition, much of it was based on emotional rather than logical grounds. The consideration uppermost in the minds of most of the critics was: how could they possibly accept the reactionary leadership of the Labour Party with its policy of class collaboration and opportunist parliamentary tactics? Actually, of course, this was no real objection, since the more the Labour rank-and-file were misled, the greater the need for an alternative leadership.

Other objections brought out in the discussion, which had the appearance of being more rational were:–

> (1) That, as part of the Labour Party, the BSP would have to bear its share of the responsibility for any betrayal of the workers' interests.

> (2) That it was hopeless to expect the BSP with its few thousand members to influence seriously the policy of a body with an affiliated membership of over a million, mainly non-socialists.

In fact these arguments rested on a whole series of incorrect assumptions, ignoring the large measure of autonomy permitted by a federal constitution, lumping together the Labour rank-and-file as a "compact reactionary mass", making no distinction between non-socialists and anti-socialists and seriously under-estimating the ability of a Marxist party to influence those with whom they came in contact. However, all these were symptoms of the disease of infantile leftism which only actual experience of working in the broad labour movement could cure.

The December conference was on a much larger scale than the one held the previous July. More delegates attended from each of the British socialist groups and there were present, in addition to the chairman and secretary of the International Bureau many distinguished foreign socialists, including Karl Kautsky, Jean Jaurès and Anatole France.

A conciliatory spirit was shown by all the groups taking part. On the instructions of their EC, the BSP delegates had stipulated that, in the event of affiliation, the party should have complete freedom of action on the following four points:–

(1) To state clearly the ultimate aims of social democracy, viz., the abolition of wage slavery and the ownership and control of all the means of making and distributing wealth with a view to establishing a democratic co-operative commonwealth.

(2) The recognition of the existence of a class war between wage-earners and the classes in possession.

(3) The obligation to aid the trade unions and other organised workers in and out of the House of Commons in all their endeavours to hold their own against the forces of capitalism.

(4) The running of BSP candidates as socialists.

Speaking on behalf of the other British groups, Keir Hardie gave a guarantee that absolute freedom of action would be permitted as regards the first three points. Concerning the fourth agreement was reached to consult the members of the respective organisations with a view to requesting the Labour Party to so modify its constitution that a candidate could describe himself as "Labour & Socialist".

The conference ended on a highly optimistic note with arrangements for the holding of a series of joint demonstrations to promote socialist unity: while the International Bureau lost no time in addressing to socialists of all shades of opinion in Britain a manifesto expressing its conviction that trade union action could end only with the abolition of capitalism, and socialist ideas must prevail in organisations that were in fact conducting the class struggle and calling for quick and resolute action to combine the socialist forces. This was supported by the issue, in February 1914, of a statement by the BSP Executive calling upon members to respond to the Bureau's appeal for the formation of a United Socialist Council and the affiliation of the party to the Labour Party.

Though these announcements carried considerable weight, they were far from sufficient to silence the opposition within the BSP, which continued to be as vocal as ever until the date of the Easter Conference.

This conference, held at the Cannon Street Hotel, was the occasion for the final debate on the unity proposals, which were introduced in the following passage from the Executive's report:–

> After very careful consideration of the proposals, we recommended their adoption by you in a Manifesto issued on February 5th supported by a Manifesto from the International Socialist Bureau... we are, therefore, arranging for adequate consideration of the whole matter at the Annual Conference and for the decision of the Party to be taken after the Conference by a referendum of members attending specially convened Branch Meetings.

In the course of the discussion on these proposals strong feeling was displayed by most of the speakers, especially the critics of the Executive. More than one of the latter tried to make capital out of Harry Quelch's last letter of protest against Labour Party affiliation and even went so far as to suggest that any decision in its favour would be a betrayal of his memory but this "argument" made little impression on the delegates.

The discussion opened with a well reasoned statement by Dan Irving who reminded the conference that, at Amsterdam nine years before, the socialists of Great Britain were called upon to recognise the fact that, as in every country, there was really but one capitalist party so, in the interests not merely of socialist theory but also of working class solidarity and in the hope of working class emancipation, socialists should strive to the utmost for that solidarity which would result in one working class party to oppose the capitalist party. In the recent discussions not an argument had been brought forward in favour of their traditional policy that had not been advanced in the past. All the prophecies that could be made as to the outcome of that policy had been made before and had failed to come true. As one of the minority who for many years had accepted a policy with which they disagreed, he concluded by appealing to all sections to abide loyally by whatever decision was reached by the majority of the members.

The main speaker for the opposition view was H. Pearse (NW Ham) who based most of his remarks on the record of the Labour group in the House of Commons. He enumerated a whole series of questions on which they had taken up an anti-working class attitude and pointed out that they were even prepared to vote against their own amendments rather than risk the defeat of the Liberal Government. He was anxious to achieve socialist unity but this must be unity of socialists. What was likely to happen, if the present proposals were adopted, was that the BSP votes would be swamped by those of the other sections.

The remaining contributors to the discussion were: T. Kennedy (Aberdeen), L. E. Quelch (H. Quelch's brother, Reading), J. Fineberg (Stepney), V. Fisher (Central), A. Lees (Rochdale), V. McEntee (Edinburgh) and H. M. Hyndman in support of the proposals and F. Walker (Deptford), J. E. Lock (Poplar), Gil Roberts (Openshaw), P. Petroff (Kentish Town), J. Jeffs (Northampton) and C. Quinn (Leyton) against.

Perhaps the most thoughtful of many effective contributions was that of Joe Fineberg of Stepney who was to play an important part in the subsequent developments of the party. He did not brush aside as of no account the arguments of the opponents of affiliation but shared their concern over the corrupting influence of the opportunist elements in the Labour movement. What he feared even more, however, was the prospect of militant socialists being isolated from the London Labour Party which was then in process of formation.

The debate on the unity proposals was followed by the appearance of the foreign delegates led by Camille Huysmans who were given a great reception. As Secretary of the International Bureau, Huysmans addressed the conference in terms appropriate to the situation. Quoting the experience of his native Belgium, be pointed out that the party there had not always been socialist but it had been found possible to transform its fair-wage conceptions into those of a party whose aim was to abolish wage-slavery. Then he added significantly "If wine is put into water the wine will not become white by the action of the water but the water will become red by the action of the wine".

The result of the members' referendum, announced on May 27th, showed a narrow majority for the unity proposals, 3,263 voting in favour and 2,410 against. Two things stand out in this connection – (1) the size of the opposition vote, notwithstanding the combined influence of the whole Executive and the International Bureau and (2) the smallness of the total vote which, allowing for a large proportion of abstentions, suggested a big drop in the party membership as compared with the 40,000 claimed in 1912.

It is also interesting to note that the most controversial of the proposals - Labour Party affiliation – was the only one actually carried into effect (though not until 1916, owing to the cancellation through war conditions of the 1915 Labour Conference). It had been assumed that, once the question of affiliation was settled, the formation of the United Socialist Council would automatically follow – which, no doubt it would have done in the absence of war. As things happened, however, it was rendered impossible by the emergence of new issues which not only created fresh divisions among British socialists but split the movement into fragments everywhere else.

Taking into consideration the special features of the British labour movement, there can be no doubt that the decision to apply for affiliation to the Labour Party was the only possible one for a body that aspired to rise above the level of a propagandist sect. The tragic irony of the situation lay in the fact that those most active in bringing it about (Hyndman, Irving, Fisher, Hunter Watts, Gorle, Kennedy etc.) were also mainly responsible, three months later, for committing the to the support of the First Imperialist World War.

Addendum in Frank Tanner's MS (originally entitled "note to page 101")

Fineberg was a young Jewish comrade whose people fled from Russia to escape Tsarist persecution. He was a profound Marxist scholar as well as one of the most popular propagandists in East London. Shortly after the revolution he returned to Russia and later did splendid work as a translator into English of the Marxist-Leninist classics.

Editors' notes

1. Tanner is mistaken here; the "Socialist Catechism" was originally the work of J. L. Joynes. In 1903 the Twentieth Century Press issued *A New Catechism of Socialism*, by Belfort Bax and Harry Quelch; this pamphlet underwent several editions. A facsimile of the 1909 edition can be found here: http://babel.hathitrust.org/cgi/pt?id=osu.32435000377382;view=1up;seq=1

2. Richard Burdon Haldane, Secretary of State for War 1906-1912, proposed and implemented wide-ranging reforms of the British army, including its reorganisation into two main parts: a territorial force for home defence, and an expeditionary force for fighting wars overseas. The formation of the territorial force was enacted by the Territorial and Reserve Forces Act, 1907.

3. The book title here refers to a compilation volume. The article cited is J. V. Stalin, "Concerning the Presentation of the National Question", published in *Pravda* on 8 May 1921, and reprinted in *Works* Vol. 5, (Moscow, 1954).

4. Caister Socialist Holiday Camp near Great Yarmouth, Norfolk, was opened by ILP member John Fletcher Dodd in 1906. It was one of the earliest holiday camps in Britain. After the war it abandoned its political aims for a wider appeal. The camp still exists, as a purely commercial concern.

5. It is hard to be sure where this addendum was supposed to go; it does not relate well to the text on page 79 of Tanner's original typescript.

Cover of pamphlet from 1908 by Zelda Kahan (later Zelda Coates), a leading figure in the SDP internationalist current.

The Socialist History Society

The Socialist History Society was founded in 1992 and includes many leading Socialist and labour historians, academic and amateur researchers, in Britain and overseas. The SHS holds regular events, public meetings and seminars, and contributes to current historical debates and controversies. We produce a range of publications, including the journal *Socialist History* and a regular Newsletter.

The SHS is the successor to the Communist Party History Group, which was established in 1946 and is now totally independent of all political parties and groups. We are engaged in and seek to encourage historical studies from a Marxist and broadly-defined left perspective. We are interested in all aspects of human history from the earliest social formations to the present day and aim for an international approach.

We are particularly interested in the various struggles of labour, of women, of progressive campaigns and peace movements around the world, as well as the history of colonial peoples, black people, and all oppressed communities seeking justice, human dignity and liberation.

Each year we produce two issues of our journal *Socialist History,* one or two historical pamphlets in our *Occasional Publications* series, and frequent members' Newsletters. We hold public lectures and seminars mainly in London. In addition, we hold special conferences, book launches and joint events with other friendly groups.

Join the Socialist History Society today!
Members receive all our serial publications for the year at no extra cost and regular mailings about our activities. Members can vote at our AGM and seek election to positions on the committee, and are encouraged to participate in other society activities.

Annual membership fees for 2015 (renewable every January):
Full UK   £25.00
Concessionary UK   £18.00
Europe full   £30.00
Europe concessionary   £24.00
Rest of world full   £35.00
Rest of world concessionary   £29.00

For details of institutional subscriptions, please e-mail the Treasurer on francis@socialisthistorysociety.co.uk.

To join the society for 2015, please send your name and address plus a cheque/PO payable to **Socialist History Society** to: SHS, 50 Elmfield Road, Balham, London SW17 8AL. You can also pay online.
Visit our websites on www.socialisthistorysociety.co.uk and www.socialist-history-journal.org.uk.